THE BRIDGE BOOK

VOLUME 2 — FOR INTERMEDIATE PLAYERS

by Frank Stewart
and Randall Baron

Drawings by Jude Goodwin

Published by
Devyn Press, Inc.
Louisville, Kentucky

Dedications

To C.H.
—F.S.
To Mary, Devyn and Dustin.
—R.S.B.

Acknowledgments

Grateful thanks to:
Betty Mattison for her patience and typesetting skills;
Pat Houington, Tony Lipka and Henry Francis for their editorial
   assistance;
Izzy Ellis and V.B.I. for their cover photography;
also to Mary Black, Mimi Maier, Bonnie Baron Pollack and
   Debbie Quire.

The reader is referred to as "he" to make the text more readable.

Printed in the United States of America.

Devyn Press, Inc.
3600 Chamberlain Lane, Suite 230
Louisville, KY 40241

ISBN 0-910791-34-1

Table of Contents

Preface

A lot of people contend that they play bridge "just for fun." While this in a way is an enviable attitude, the authors' view is that *the better you play, the more fun you'll have.* Now that you know some of the fundamentals of good bridge, you are ready to learn more about playing the game well.

Much of the material in this book reviews and expands upon basic concepts. However, there is much more to bridge than the application of rules. This is a thinking person's game. Problems crop up that require logical thinking and deductive reasoning.

Therefore, the opening section of each chapter shows you something about a good player's thought processes when he faces a problem situation with no rules to guide him. This material is intended to serve as inspiration — to show you that bridge is a beautifully logical game, and to suggest that the time you spend learning to play well is well spent. At the end of each chapter there are quizzes to let you test your comprehension of the material.

The potential rewards for those who master the game are great. At the least, you will have a stimulating way of entertaining yourself and a means of making friends wherever you go. If you are more ambitious, organized tournament competition can lead all the way to the world championship!

Good luck. Enjoy yourself.

*FINDING A QUEEN DOESN'T
HAVE TO MAKE YOUR HEAD SPIN.*

Chapter 1

THINKING: HOW TO GUESS A QUEEN
REVIEW OF THE POINT COUNT
RESPONDING TO NOTRUMP OPENINGS

THINKING: HOW TO GUESS A QUEEN

Suppose you have to play this combination of cards:

K J x

A 10 x

How would you try to make three tricks? Your best shot is to finesse through the opponent you think has the missing queen. Now a slightly different example:

K J x x x

A 10 x x

The odds here slightly favor playing "for the drop" by cashing the ace-king.

Of course, the best way to deal with this type of problem is to figure out where that missing queen is, and a good player will often know where the queen is hiding. Some people seem to think that an expert is gifted with magic powers when it comes to locating a missing card. Quite often we have heard people say, "I'll bet you know what everybody at the table has after the first trick, don't you?" That isn't true; sometimes we don't know what everybody has even after the play is over. But we can try to locate a missing queen, and we don't carry a crystal ball around with us. There are very simple ways to discover what we want to know— so simple, in fact, that anybody can use them. Look at this hand:

♠ Q 10 x x
♡ K 10 x
◊ Q x x
♣ A Q x

♠ A K 9 x x
♡ A J x
◊ x x
♣ J 10 x

You are South. East dealt and passed, you opened 1 ♠, and you and partner got to 4 ♠. The opening lead is the ◊ J, which holds the first trick, and West continues with another diamond. East wins the ◊ K this time and tries to cash the ◊ A. You can ruff this trick.

Next you draw trumps. There is no reason not to. The trumps split evenly. East has J-x and West has two small trumps.

Now you can play on your other suits. There are finesses to take in both clubs and hearts. **Which finesse should you take first?** Right, you play clubs first. In hearts, you have an option about which way to finesse so you should save that play till the last minute. In clubs, though, you just have to hope the king is in the right place.

You lead the ♣ J and play low from dummy. East wins the king and leads back a club. Now you must figure out the heart suit to make your contract. **How should you guess it?**

This is *no guess* if you've been paying attention and counting. In the play so far, East has showed the ◊ A and ◊ K, the ♣ K, and the ♠ J. How many points is that? Right, 11. **Now who has the ♡ Q?**

Right, *West* has the ♡ Q. If East had it, he would have had 13 high-card points and presumably would have opened the bidding! One of the ways you can place a missing card is to *draw an inference* from what happened (or didn't happen) in the bidding. It may strike you as a difficult proposition to keep track of everything that went on in the play, but really all we did on that hand was concentrate a little and count to 13. Many of the techniques a good player uses to figure out what everybody has are *very simple in principle*.

How about another hand:

♠ J x x x x
♡ K 10 x
♢ A J
♣ J x x

♠ K Q 10 x x
♡ A J x
♢ Q x
♣ Q x x

This time *West opened the bidding* 1 ♣ , but the opponents bid no more after that. You and partner took over and wound up in 4 ♠ . The opening lead is the ♣ A.

After winning the first trick, West continues with the ♣ K and another club. Luckily for you, East has to follow suit all three times and you win the third trick. You lead the ♠ K, since again you have no reason to delay drawing trumps. West wins the ace (which doesn't surprise you, since he opened and rates to have most of the missing high cards) and he shifts to a diamond. Of course, you play dummy's jack. You expect the diamond finesse to win since West opened the bidding, and sure enough, the jack holds.

So now you can finish drawing trumps. As it happens, West had all three of the missing trumps. After two more rounds of spades, you can cash your ♢ A. Both opponents follow low; West still has the king.

So now you have to guess the hearts. This is the same position you faced on the first hand. **How would you guess it?**

West had three spades to the ace and three or four clubs to the ace-king. There is only one club out at this point. So West had six or seven black cards. How many red cards did he have then? Six or seven! Now, **how would you think his red cards would be divided?** They should be divided fairly evenly — 3-3, or 4-2, or 4-3. Remember that West opened the bidding in a suit of only four cards (at most), so you wouldn't expect him to have a longer suit anywhere. The point is that West should have a hand that is relatively *balanced*. **How many points have you seen in the West hand?** ♣ A and ♣ K, ♢ K, ♠ A. That's 14. **What if West had the ♡ Q?**

Right, with the ♡ Q in addition to his other values and a balanced hand, West would have had a classic *1 NT* opening. So *East* should have the ♡ Q.

Counting the opponents' high-card points is a simple way to find out something about what they have. Another source of information is the *way the opponents defend*. You know the opponents will bid and play logically. Their chances of beating you will be slim if they just play at random. On defense, they will have a definite purpose behind some of the plays they make. If you can figure out what they are thinking, it may help you plan *your* play. Here's an illustration:

    ♠ J x x x
    ♡ K x
    ◇ Q x x
    ♣ K 10 x x

    ♠ K Q 10 x x
    ♡ x x
    ◇ A
    ♣ A J x x x

East dealt and opened 1 ♡. You overcalled 1 ♠ and got to 4 ♠. The opening lead is a heart, and dummy's ♡ K turns out to be worth nothing. East wins two heart tricks with the ace and queen. Next, East cashes his ace of trumps and gets out of the lead safely with a low trump. West follows, so all the trumps are in. All you have to worry about is the club situation.

Say you play a low club to dummy's king. Both opponents follow low. Now you lead a club back toward your hand and East plays the last low club. You can either finesse your ♣ J at this point, playing opening bidder for the missing queen, or go up with the ♣ A, hoping that the queen will drop on your left. **What are your feelings?**

Suppose you try counting points here. East had the ♡ A and ♡ Q and the ♠ A. **Would he have to have the ♣ Q for his opening?** No, he could have the ◇ K and no ♣ Q, and he would still have enough to open. Counting points doesn't give the answer in this case.

Instead we will draw an inference from what has happened in the *play*. Suppose you choose to finesse your ♣ J now. You would be playing East for Q-x-x. So you would be assuming that West had a singleton. Now, put yourself in West's place and think with his mind for a minute. You are defending 4 ♠, you have heard your partner open the bidding and you know he has a good hand. **Suppose you were looking at a singleton club. How would you defend the hand?**

8

Notice that the opponents could always have defeated you if West had a singleton club. He could have led his singleton and taken a ruff when East got in with the ♠A. Since none of this happened, the chances are that West *doesn't have* a singleton. The ♣Q should drop if you put up your ace.

RESPONDING TO NOTRUMP OPENINGS

Every bid you make has a meaning. Through the information you and partner exchange, it is possible to tell how much *strength* your partnership has, so that you know *how high* to bid; also, whether a good trump suit, or *fit*, is available.

Let's review some important numbers:

POINT-COUNT REQUIREMENTS
FOR VARIOUS CONTRACTS:

For game in notrump or a major suit . . . . . . about 26 points
For game in a minor suit . . . . about 29 points
For a small slam . . . . about 33 points
For a grand slam . . . . about 37 points
For a partscore . . . . from 20-25 points

TO MAKE A SUIT TRUMPS AT LEAST AN EIGHT-CARD FIT IS DESIRED. If you can uncover a bigger fit, fine. A very strong seven-card fit may do in a pinch, but you will usually have trouble making a trump suit work to your advantage if the opponents have almost as many trumps as your side.

In figuring the point-count value of your hand, count points for your high cards according to the 4-3-2-1 scale and add points for certain distributional features. Long cards are potential tricks in any contract and are therefore an asset. In addition, your *short* suits *may become useful* for a trump contract *if* partner bids some other suit that you can support. You do *not* count points for your short suits when you first pick up your hand. The way the bidding develops will determine whether your short suits are assets or liabilities. In valuing your hand for play at notrump, of course, short suits are not a consideration.

Responding to notrump openings is a good place to start a bidding discussion because it is a very simple part of the bidding system. That's because an opening bid in notrump is such a well-defined bid.

Take a look:

> To open 1 NT, you need — 16-18 high-card points, balanced pattern
>
> To open 2 NT, you need — 22-24 high-card points, balanced pattern
>
> To open 3 NT, you need — 25-27 high-card points, balanced pattern

"Balanced pattern" means your hand contains no singletons or voids and no more than one doubleton. There are three possible patterns: 4-3-3-3; 4-4-3-2; 5-3-3-2. When we speak of a "balanced" hand, we mean only that the *distribution* is balanced, not that the hand has honors in every suit. Any time you have a balanced hand and 16-18 high-card points, you should open 1 NT. It's a good descriptive bid. (On the rare occasions when your high cards are concentrated in just two suits, you might decide to treat your hand as a two-suiter and open in a suit.)

When your partner opens in notrump, all you must do is add your points to the ones he showed and you can tell how high to bid. And, since you know that partner has a tolerance for every suit, you can often look at your hand and tell whether you belong in notrump or in a suit. The principle of notrump bidding: *Responder is the "captain" of the partnership and must take the initiative in placing the contract.*

Let's look at some of the options you as responder have when you hear a 1 NT opening from partner. Suppose, to begin with, that you have a *balanced* hand and you might as well stay in notrump. The only question is, at what level?

1. ♠ K x x
    ♡ Q x x
    ◊ J x x x
    ♣ x x x

    Pass. Your side has 24 points at most, not enough to consider game.

2. ♠ K x x
    ♡ Q x x
    ◊ A J x x
    ♣ J x x

    Bid 3 NT. You cannot do less when you *know* your side has enough points for game.

3. ♠ Q x   Bid 3 NT. Don't bother to mention the
    ♡ x x x   clubs. You prefer to play the *nine*-trick
    ◊ Q x x   game, not the *11*-trick club game. If your
    ♣ A K J x x   suit were a major, you might mention it
                         — ten tricks wouldn't be so bad.

4. ♠ Q x   Bid 3 NT. Our aversion to minor-suit
    ♡ x x   games is so strong that we strain to play
    ◊ A K J x x x   3 NT instead with any excuse at all. This
    ♣ x x x   is *almost* a balanced hand, and the
                         diamonds will take tricks in notrump just
as well as at a diamond contract. It's a good gamble to raise to the
notrump game.

5. ♠ K x x   Bid *2 NT*. This *invites* partner to go on to
    ♡ Q x x   3 NT if he has closer to 18 points for his
    ◊ A x x x   notrump opening.
    ♣ x x x

6. ♠ K x x   Bid 6 NT. This is what the combined
    ♡ A Q x   hands rate to produce, so don't chicken
    ◊ K J x x   out. Accept your responsibility to place
    ♣ A x x   the contract. It's up to you, remember.

7. ♠ K x x   Bid *4 NT*. This *invites* partner to go on
    ♡ A Q x   to 6 NT with closer to 18 points for his
    ◊ K x x x x   notrump opening. In this situation, a 4 NT
    ♣ A x   bid is just a raise of notrump and *not* an
                         ace-asking bid. Notice that if partner ac-
                         cepts, you cannot be off two aces.

Now suppose your hand is unbalanced:

8. ♠ J x x x x x   Bid 2 ♠. A response of two of a suit (ex-
    ♡ x   cept 2 ♣, which is a special bid) is a
    ◊ x x x   *signoff*. Partner must respect your judg-
    ♣ x x x   ment in placing the contract and pass. It
                         may look strange to bid at all with so few
points. But your hand will not take a single trick at notrump, while
it will take several if spades is trumps.

9. ♠ K Q x x x x   Bid 4♠. This is what you think you can
    ♡ x   make. Remember our principle: Re-
    ◊ A J x   sponder must make sure the proper level
    ♣ x x x   is reached. You have enough strength to
try a game, and there must be an eight-
card fit in spades — partner couldn't open 1 NT without at least two.

10. ♠ K Q x x x   You could raise to 3 NT, but spades might
    ♡ x x   be better. The opponents might establish
    ◊ A J x   and cash some long cards in one of your
    ♣ x x x   weak suits at a notrump contract. The play
would be safer with spades as trumps, and
a *major*-suit game is only ten tricks. Bid 3♠. This bid shows a good
hand, but says your suit is not so good that you can insist that it be
trumps. Partner can *raise* you with three-card support or better, or
he can go back to 3 NT without support. Compare with #9, where
you had a *six*-card suit and were willing to play 4♠ opposite *whatever*
support partner had.

11. ♠ x x   The response of three of a suit is most
    ♡ J x   often used to offer partner a choice be-
    ◊ A K Q x x x   tween 3 NT and four of a *major* suit. The
    ♣ x x x   advice on hands like this one, remember,
was to bid 3 NT, avoiding the 11-trick
minor-suit game.

12. ♠ x   Bid 3♣. This time your hand is very dis-
    ♡ A x x x   tributional — 5♣ or 6♣ could be the
    ◊ x x   correct contract. Your 3♣ bid suggests
    ♣ A K J x x x   doubts about notrump and invites partner
to raise.

RESPONDING TO 1 NT

With 0-7 points	PASS with balanced pattern, or BID TWO OF A SUIT (except clubs) with at least five cards in the suit. This is a weak action and partner must pass.
With 8-9 points	RAISE TO 2 NT with balanced pattern.
With 10-14 points	RAISE TO 3 NT with balanced pattern or BID FOUR OF A MAJOR SUIT with a six-card suit.
With 10 points up	BID THREE OF A SUIT with a good five-card suit or longer. This is forcing (to game) and asks partner to support your suit if possible.
With 15-16 points	RAISE TO 4 NT with balanced pattern.
With 17-18 points	RAISE TO 6 NT with balanced pattern.
With 19-20 points	RAISE TO 5 NT with balanced pattern. (This bid invites a grand slam. Partner *must* bid at least 6 NT.)
With 21 points up	BID 7 NT.

In responding to a *2 NT* opening, apply the same principle as in responding to *1 NT*. Responder must make sure the right level is reached.

13. ♠ J x x
    ♡ K x x
    ♢ x x x
    ♣ x x x x

Bid 3 NT. You don't need much to raise to game opposite a hand worth at least 22 high-card points.

14. ♠ K x x
    ♡ A x x
    ♢ K J x
    ♣ x x x x

Bid 6 NT.

Over 2 NT, *any suit bid at the three level is forcing.* (3♣ is a special bid.) Opener should raise or go back to 3 NT depending on whether he has support for responder's suit.

15. ♠ K Q x x x
    ♡ x x
    ♢ J x x
    ♣ x x x

Bid 3 ♠.

13

16. ♠ x   Bid 4♡.
     ♡ J 10 x x x x
     ◇ A x x
     ♣ x x x

In the next chapter, we will see that responder has one other option over a notrump opening. This is the *Stayman Convention,* a useful and widely-played special bid.

*YOUR PARTNERSHIP CAN CREATE A MASTERPIECE
WITH ACCURATE NOTRUMP BIDDING.*

TEST YOUR COMPREHENSION OF THE MATERIAL IN THIS CHAPTER:

(1) You are declarer with these cards in 4 ♡ :

♠ A x x x
♡ J 10 x x
◊ K x x
♣ x x

♠ J x
♡ A Q 9 x x
◊ A Q x
♣ K J x

You opened 1 ♡ after three passes, West overcalled 1 ♠, North raised to 2 ♡, you invited game with 3 ♡, and North went on to 4 ♡. West led the ♠ K. You won the ace and took a heart finesse, losing to West's king. He cashed his ♠ Q and continued with the ♠ 10. East showed out and you ruffed. You drew the rest of the trumps and led a club from dummy, East playing small. Do you play your ♣ K or ♣ J?

(2) You are declarer with these cards in 5 ◊ :

♠ x x x
♡ K 10 x x
◊ x x x
♣ A x x

♠ J
♡ A J x
◊ K Q J 10 x x x
♣ K x

West	North	East	South
1 ♠	Pass	Pass	Double
Pass	2 ♡	Pass	4 ◊
Pass	5 ◊	(All Pass)	

West led the ♠ K and continued with the queen, which you ruffed. The ◊ K was won by East's ace and you ruffed the spade return. After drawing the rest of the trumps, how do you attack the heart suit?

SOLUTIONS:

(1) Play the ♣K. West would have opened the bidding with the ♣A in addition to his five good spades and his ♡K.

(2) Finesse West for the ♡Q. East would have responded to the opening bid with the ♡Q in addition to the ◊A.

QUIZ ON RESPONDING TO NOTRUMP OPENINGS:

Partner opens 1 NT (16-18 balanced). What is your response with:

1. ♠ K x
    ♡ A x x
    ◊ K Q x x x
    ♣ Q J x

2. ♠ K x
    ♡ J x x
    ◊ K x x x
    ♣ x x x x

3. ♠ x x
    ♡ A x x
    ◊ J x x
    ♣ K x x x x

4. ♠ K Q x
    ♡ A Q x
    ◊ A K x x
    ♣ Q J x

5. ♠ x x
    ♡ A Q x x x
    ◊ K Q x
    ♣ x x x

6. ♠ J x
    ♡ x x x
    ◊ A Q x x x
    ♣ K x x

7. ♠ K Q x
    ♡ A x x
    ◊ K x x x
    ♣ K x x

8. ♠ x
    ♡ J 10 x x x x
    ◊ A x x
    ♣ K x x

9. ♠ x x x x x x x
    ♡ x x x
    ◊ x
    ♣ x x x

10. ♠ A x
    ♡ K x x
    ◊ A Q x x
    ♣ K J x x

11. ♠ —
    ♡ K x x
    ◊ Q x x x
    ♣ A Q x x x x

12. ♠ A K x x x
    ♡ x x
    ◊ A J x x
    ♣ K x

16

13. ♠ A K x   14. ♠ x
    ♡ K x x   ♡ Q x x x x
    ◊ K J x x   ◊ J x x x
    ♣ A J x   ♣ x x x

15. ♠ x
    ♡ A Q x x x x
    ◊ A x x
    ♣ A J x

Partner opens 2 NT (22-24 balanced). What is your response with:

1. ♠ K x x   2. ♠ K x x
   ♡ K x x   ♡ A x x
   ◊ x x x x   ◊ Q x x x
   ♣ x x x   ♣ J x x

3. ♠ x x   4. ♠ A x
   ♡ Q J x x x   ♡ x x x
   ◊ K x x   ◊ K J x x
   ♣ x x x   ♣ K x x x

5. ♠ x x
   ♡ Q x x
   ◊ x x x
   ♣ A x x x x

SOLUTIONS:

1. 4 NT	6. 3 NT	11. 3♣
2. Pass	7. 4 NT	12. 3♠
3. 2 NT	8. 4♡	13. 5 NT
4. 7 NT	9. 2♠	14. 2♡
5. 3♡	10. 6 NT	15. 6♡ (or 3♡)

1. 3 NT	3. 3♡	5. 3NT
2. 4 NT	4. 6 NT	

Chapter 2

THINKING:
FINE POINTS OF HAND EVALUATION
THE STAYMAN CONVENTION

THINKING: FINE POINTS OF HAND EVALUATION

When you first began to play bridge, you were introduced to the point-count method of hand evaluation. The point-count is a way of translating the *trick-taking* power of your hand into an easy-to-work-with *numerical* value. Since the 4-3-2-1 count has the virtue of *simplicity,* it is universally cherished.

The more you play bridge, however, the more you realize that many factors determine the true worth of a bridge hand. Alfred Sheinwold, in his best-selling book *Five Weeks to Winning Bridge,* wryly and accurately observed that the real value of your hand may depend on extraneous factors like how good a player your partner is, who in the game has had one drink too many, and so forth. Sheinwold meant that hand evaluation is difficult, and few hard and fast rules are accepted as the gospel truth.

The *number* of points your hand contains may not indicate its true value. Good hand evaluation means realizing when the point-count is untrustworthy. Instead of dwelling on points and rules, we want to look at some of the less obvious factors a good player considers in deciding how much he should bid.

1. **How many points is this hand worth when you first pick it up?**

   ♠ —
   ♡ Q x x x x
   ◊ K J x x
   ♣ A x x x

There is a popular but dangerous practice in valuing hands like this — adding points for the void suit to begin with. Long and bitter experience at bridge teaches that partner can be counted on to bid your void suit several times. A void in partner's suit is anything but an asset. However, if your partner happened to bid one of the suits you have support for, then the value of this hand, the number of tricks will produce with partner's suit as trumps, would increase dramatically.

NOTE THIS WELL. You *cannot* count points for *short* suits when you first pick up your hand. The value of your short suits depends on how the bidding develops. You add extra points for shortness only when you have support for a suit your partner has bid or when partner supports one of your suits. The value of your shortness depends on, among other things, how good your support for partner's bid suit is, or how good his is for yours.

Since a *long, strong suit* is a real and obvious source of tricks you may count extra points for *length* right away. You must be careful here also, though. In trying to decide how many points to add for long suits, you must assess your chances of making tricks with your long cards. A *poor suit* may be hard to establish. A long suit in a poor *hand* may also be hard to establish, because of the lack of entries.

2. **Which of these two hands would you rather have?** Notice that each contains 13 high-card points.

(a)   ♠ Q J x   (b)   ♠ A K x
        ♡ K J x x   ♡ x x x x
        ◊ K J x   ◊ x x x
        ♣ Q x x   ♣ A Q x

(b) is clearly better. Aces and kings are cards that will take tricks regardless of which side is declaring. They are worth a little *more* than the point-count values assigned to them. Any time you have a hand with lots of "primary values," your hand is really worth more than you think it is. Queens and jacks are *overvalued* on our 4-3-2-1 scale, however.

3. (a)   ♠ A Q x x x   (b)   ♠ x x x x x
        ♡ A K x x   ♡ x x x x
        ◊ x x   ◊ A Q
        ♣ x x   ♣ A K

(a) is better. It is better to have your high cards along with your length, so that the long cards can be established more easily.

4. (a)   ♠ A x x x   (b)   ♠ A K x x
         ♡ K x x   ♡ x x x
         ◊ J x   ◊ x x
         ♣ A x x x   ♣ A J x x

(b) is better. You prefer your high cards to *complement* each other. The ♠ K in (b) is a sure trick when supported by the ace, and the ♣ J in (b) has a better chance of being a trick with the ace to back it up. Do you think these are both "12-point" hands?

5.   ♠ Q x
        ♡ K J x
        ◊ J 9 x x
        ♣ A 10 x x

Partner has opened 1 ♠. **Would a 2 ♡ overcall by your right-hand opponent increase the value of this hand?** Yes, certainly. Your right-hand opponent is likely to have the top hearts for his bid, so your king-jack is worth two tricks, as though you had the ace-king! You should bid *3 NT*.

6.   ♠ x x x x
        ♡ A 9 x x
        ◊ A Q 10 x
        ♣ x

The bidding has proceeded:

	(YOU)		
East	*South*	*West*	*North*
1 ♠	Pass	2 ♠	3 ♡
3 ♠	?		

What should you bid?
Forget about your point-count on this hand for a minute and think instead in terms of tricks. How do you think the play will go if hearts is trumps? What winners and losers do you have?

Partner has at most one spade on this bidding and may have none at all. He should have an excellent heart suit to come in by himself at the three level. He may have the ◊ K, but if he does not, **which opponent would you expect to have it?** Right, the hand that opened the bidding. So if partner has as much as the ◊ J, or if he has only two diamonds, there will be no losers in that suit. There is only one club loser, and none if partner holds the ace. You know partner has some high cards for his bid and they aren't in spades, so he may have the ♣A. Let's give partner a hand with 10 high-card points opposite our 10:

♠ —
♡ K Q x x x x
♦ J 9 x
♣ A x x x

If he has that hand, how many tricks will he take in hearts? All 13, right? You simply have no losers! We would bid 6♡, since it seems like a good gamble.

Distribution can be a powerful factor in winning tricks. If two hands are balanced, it takes about 26 high-card points to make a notrump game, and the point-count is a good way of deciding how high to bid. But when you have very distributional hands, the *number* of points you have can be secondary. The emphasis shifts to *which* high cards you have and how good your trump fit is. On this example, 13 tricks can be made at hearts, with only 20 high-card points, because your points are just the right ones. Long suits and distribution provide tricks.

7. (a)   ♠ K Q x x x   (b)   ♠ A x x x x
          ♡ x x x   ♡ Q x x
          ♦ x x   ♦ K x
          ♣ K J x   ♣ x x x

Partner opened 1♡, you chose a 1♠ response and he rebid 2♦. Which hand do you prefer? Hand (b) is better. You would rather have high cards *in the suits partner has bid,* where they will help him establish his long cards.

8. (a)   ♠ K x x x
          ♡ K x x
          ♦ Q x x x
          ♣ J x

Partner opens 1♠, your right-hand opponent overcalls 2♦, you raise to 2♠, left-hand opponent raises to 3♦, your partner bids 3♠. How many points is this hand worth? Not much more than 7, probably. The ◊ Q will be useless to partner, since he will be trumping diamonds right away.

9. Here's another example. You can see that certain high cards can be more useful than others. Two good players missed a laydown game on these cards.

♠ x x　　　　　　　　　　　♠ x x x x
♡ A K J x x　　　　　　　　♡ Q x x x
◊ A x x x　　　　　　　　　◊ K Q x
♣ A x　　　　　　　　　　　♣ x x

The bidding went: 1 ♡, 2 ♡, 3 ♡, pass. How could this game have been reached?

Notice how well these hands "fit" together. The high cards complement each other perfectly, so that game can be made, perhaps even with an overtrick, with only 23 high-card points. The key is East's diamond holding; he has just what West needs to cover several of his losers.

The way to reach game is for West to try for game by bidding *3 ◊*. 3 ◊ must show interest in game, since West would not bid at all over 2 ♡ if he knew that no game was possible. A 3 ♡ rebid by West forces East to make a decision based only on *how many* points he has, while *3 ◊* allows East to attach extra significance to *cards in his partner's second suit.*

So the bidding should go:

West	East
1 ♡	2 ♡
3 ◊ *	4 ♡ **

*"I'm interested in game, especially if you have help in diamonds as well as hearts."
**"I only have a minimum raise, but it looks as if my points are just the right ones."

Note that if East's hand were:

♠ x x
♡ Q x x x
◊ x x x x
♣ K Q x

(the same hand with the suits changed around), he would know to reject partner's try for game and return to *3♡*. He has a minimum raise and his diamond help is terrible.

REVIEW OF NOTRUMP RESPONSES

We saw that, if the opening bid is 1 NT, *responder* becomes "captain" of the partnership. Since he knows that opener has precisely 16-18 high-card points, he can easily figure the *combined* values of the partnership and decide how many tricks are likely. Also, since he knows that opener has a tolerance for every suit, he can often tell whether the contract should be played in notrump or in a suit.

So it is *responder's* duty to take the initiative in placing the contract. Let's look at a couple of example situations:

1. ♠ J x x x x x
   ♡ x x x
   ◇ x
   ♣ x x x

   If partner opens 1 NT here, you *sign off* in 2♠. Partner cannot bid further — he must respect your decision.

2. ♠ K Q x x x x
   ♡ A x
   ◇ J x x x
   ♣ x

   This time you jump to *4♠*. Remember that at least an eight-card "fit" is desired before you make a suit the trump suit. Here you must have at least eight spades since partner couldn't open 1 NT without at least two of them.

3. ♠ K Q x x x
   ♡ A x
   ◇ J x x x
   ♣ x x

   You respond *3♠*. Partner will raise to 4♠ with three-card support or better, but will return to notrump with only two spades. This way you can play in spades when you have a "fit" (maybe a 5-3 fit) but notrump otherwise.

4. ♠ K Q x x
   ♡ x x
   ◇ J x x x
   ♣ A x x

   You could raise to 3 NT, but there could be a "fit," this time a *4-4* fit, in spades. It is often better to play with a trump suit. Possession of some trumps can help you *control* the play and may provide some *extra tricks*. It would be nice if you could find out if *partner also had four spades*. How can you do this?

23

THE STAYMAN CONVENTION:

The problem is that *you can't bid any number of spades.* 2♠ would be a signoff, 3♠ would invite partner to raise you with only three cards, and a 4♠ response is clearly a shot in the dark with only four spades. To handle this situation, we need a *gadget.*

A *CONVENTION* at bridge is a bid with an artificial meaning. In devising a convention, knowledgeable players decide it is more useful to assign an *artificial* meaning to a bid than to have it retain its *natural* meaning.

The STAYMAN CONVENTION became popular about 1950. It is a response of *2♣* to 1 NT. (Over a 2 NT opening a *3♣* response is STAYMAN.) If you and your partner agree to play this convention, then a response of 2♣ to 1 NT says nothing about what responder has in clubs. (Responder may not have a single club, in fact!) 2♣ *merely asks opener if he has a four-card major suit.* It's like a coded message.

Up to now, we've said that a response of two of a suit is weak and requests partner to pass. 2♣ is almost *universally* played as an exception to this. Every good bridge player uses the STAYMAN CONVENTION.

Over 2♣, opener bids 2♡ or 2♠ if he has four cards in either suit. (There is disagreement among experts over what opener should do if he has *both* major suits — many players bid their stronger major suit first.) If opener has no major to show, he bids 2♢. This is another part of the code. It says nothing about opener's diamonds, just as the 2♣ STAYMAN response bears no relation to responder's clubs. A 2♢ rebid by opener merely denies a major suit.

TAKE THE MYSTERY OUT OF BIDDING BY USING STAYMAN.

After responder finds out whether opener has a major suit, he places the contract as usual. Let's look at some example auctions. In each case, your partner has opened 1 NT:

5. ♠ A J x x   Respond 2♣, STAYMAN. If opener can
   ♡ x x   show four spades, bid game in spades.
   ◊ K x x x   Otherwise, bid 3 NT.
   ♣ K x x

6. ♠ A J x x   Respond 2♣. If opener shows four
   ♡ x x   spades, raise to *3♠* (invitational). Other-
   ◊ K x x x   wise, bid 2 *NT* inviting game.
   ♣ J x x

7. ♠ A x x x   Pass. If you use Stayman, you imply
   ♡ x x   interest in game. You are too weak to be
   ◊ K x x x   interested in game here. You must take
   ♣ x x x   your chances in 1 NT.

8. ♠ A Q x x   Use Stayman. If you locate a major-suit
   ♡ K Q x x   fit, bid *six* of your suit. Otherwise, raise
   ◊ A x x   to 4 NT, inviting a slam in notrump.
   ♣ J x

9. ♠ A Q x x x   This kind of hand would be a real head-
   ♡ x x   ache without Stayman. You are too strong
   ◊ Q x x x   to sign off with 2♠, since there is a
   ♣ x x   chance for game; but you aren't strong
   enough to force to game with a *3♠* re-
sponse. Start with 2♣ (game interest, at least). If partner rebids 2♠,
you raise (to three). If his rebid is 2◊ or 2♡, you continue with
2♠. You have shown invitational values (8-9 points) and you suggest *five* spades, since you would have no reason to bid spades at
all on this auction with only four of them. (You would return to
notrump instead.) Your partner can now place the contract.

10. ♠ x x x   You would love to sign off with 2♣, but
    ♡ x x x   you cannot. Partner will think you are
    ◊ x   using Stayman. Most players handle this
    ♣ J 10 x x x x   problem by bidding 2♣ *anyway*, which
    will temporarily deceive their partner. But
after partner shows a major or bids 2◊, they bid *3♣*, which says,

"I was only kidding, I really have a weak hand with clubs." If you want to sign off in clubs, you must go to the three level (by steps) to do it.

11. ♠ J x x x With this hand, you can use Stayman in
    ♡ Q x x x an unusual way. Respond 2 ♣, planning
    ◊ J x x x x to pass any rebid by opener (even 2 ◊ !).
    ♣ —

Suppose the opponents interfere with your plan to use Stayman. What do you do then?

12. ♠ K Q x x Partner opens 1 NT, and you are about
    ♡ A x x x to respond 2 ♣ when your right-hand op-
    ◊ x x ponent overcalls 2 ◊ ! You can no longer
    ♣ J x x bid 2 ♣, but there is another way to use
    Stayman — with *a bid of the opponent's*
suit. (You could hardly want to bid 3 ◊ *to play;* if you had diamonds, you would *double* the opponents for penalties.)

Let's look at a couple of Stayman sequences from opener's side of the table.

13. ♠ A K x x Partner responds 2 ♣ to your 1 NT open-
    ♡ K Q x x ing. Suppose you decide to bid 2 ♠. Part-
    ◊ Q x ner now says 3 NT. You would bid *4♡*.
    ♣ K x x You know partner has a major suit since
    he used Stayman, and if he wasn't in
    terested in spades, he must have hearts.

14. ♠ A K x x Partner responds 2 ♣ to your 1 NT open-
    ♡ K Q x x ing. Suppose you decide to bid 2 ♠. Part-
    ◊ A Q ner now says 2 NT. You jump to *4♡*.
    ♣ x x x Partner has invitational strength and
    hearts, so you accept his try for game. If
your ♡ Q were a small heart, you would bid just *3♡*.

15. ♠ K Q x Partner responds 2 ♣ to your 1 NT open-
    ♡ x x ing. You bid 2 ◊, denying a major, and
    ◊ A K x x partner now says 2 ♠. You would bid
    ♣ A J x x *4♠*. Partner has shown invitational
    strength with five spades, and you have
a maximum hand and good help for his suit.

26

TEST YOUR COMPREHENSION OF THE MATERIAL IN THIS CHAPTER:

QUIZ ON FINE POINTS OF HAND EVALUATION:

1. You opened 1 ♡ and partner responded 1 NT. To raise to 2 NT, would you rather have:

   (a) ♠ A x x   (b) ♠ A x x
   ♡ A K 9 8 x   ♡ Q J 10 9 8
   ◊ Q J 10   ◊ A K x
   ♣ K x   ♣ K x

2. The opponents bid and raised spades, and your partner over-called in hearts. Which hand would you prefer to raise him?

   (a) ♠ —   (b) ♠ —
   ♡ x x x   ♡ x x x x x
   ◊ K x x x x   ◊ K x x x
   ♣ A x x x x   ♣ A x x x

3. Partner opened 1 ♠, you raised to 2 ♠. Now he tries for game with 3 ♠. To accept, would you prefer:

   (a) ♠ Q x x x   (b) ♠ A x x x
   ♡ x x   ♡ x x
   ◊ A x x x   ◊ Q x x x
   ♣ Q x x   ♣ Q x x

4. You open 1 ♣, left-hand opponent overcalls 1 ♡, and partner bids 1 ♠. You rebid 1 NT and are raised to 2 NT. To go on to 3 NT, would you prefer:

   (a) ♠ J x   (b) ♠ A x
   ♡ A x x   ♡ Q J x
   ◊ K J x x   ◊ x x x x
   ♣ K Q x x   ♣ A Q J x

5.   Your partner opened 1♠. Which hand would you prefer?

(a)   ♠ A x x x   (b)   ♠ A x x x
      ♡ K x x   ♡ x x x
      ◇ x   ◇ K
      ♣ x x x x x   ♣ x x x x x

6.   Your partner opened 1♠, right-hand opponent bid 2◇, you
     raised to 2♠, left-hand opponent came in with 3♣. Partner
     now tried for game with 3♡. Which hand would you prefer
     to accept?

(a)   ♠ K x x x   (b)   ♠ K x x x
      ♡ Q x   ♡ J x
      ◇ K x x   ◇ Q x x x
      ♣ x x x x   ♣ K x x

7.   Which of these two hands do you prefer?

(a)   ♠ A Q x x   (b)   ♠ K J x x
      ♡ x x   ♡ Q J x
      ◇ x x x   ◇ Q J x
      ♣ A K x x   ♣ Q J x

8.   Which of these two hands do you prefer?

(a)   ♠ A K J x x   (b)   ♠ J x x x x
      ♡ A Q x x   ♡ A x x x
      ◇ x x x   ◇ K Q x
      ♣ x   ♣ A

SOLUTIONS:

1. (b) is the better hand. You prefer to have intermediate cards in your long suit, so that the long cards can surely be established.

2. (b) is the better hand. The principle here is that the worth of your short suits depends on how good your support for partner's suit is. On hand (a), your support is so minimal that partner may have a hard time taking advantage of your shortness. A trump opening lead will be damaging; or, partner may not be able to get off dummy safely after just one spade ruff.

3. (a) is slightly better. The ♠Q in (a) is bound to be a helpful card, with partner known to have spade length. The value of the ◇Q in (b) is unknown.

4. Prefer hand (b). The problem with (a) is that you lack aces, always a worry when the opponents have a long suit they will try to set up against your notrump contract. When you lack aces, your opponents may have the entries to set up the heart suit before you can get *your* tricks established. *Good hand evaluation often means visualizing how the play will go.*

5. (a) is the better hand. *Singleton* honors are of questionable value.

6. (a) is the better hand. The ◇K is well-positioned, behind the diamond bidder, and the ♡Q is a good card. On (b), the ◇Q is probably worthless, and the ♣K, in front of left-hand opponent's club bid, is suspect.

7. (a) is much the better hand, even though both hands contain 13 points in high cards. Note the Quick-Trick structure.

8. (a) is much the better hand — the high cards are located in the longer suits.

QUIZ ON USING THE STAYMAN CONVENTION:

I. Partner has opened 1 NT. What is your response with:

1. ♠ K Q x x   2. ♠ K Q x x
    ♡ x x   ♡ K x
    ◇ K Q x x   ◇ J x x x
    ♣ x x x   ♣ x x x

3. ♠ K Q x x   4. ♠ K Q x x x
    ♡ x x   ♡ x x
    ◇ J x x x   ◇ A x x
    ♣ x x x   ♣ Q x x

5. ♠ K Q x x x   6. ♠ 10 x x x
   ♡ A x x x   ♡ Q J x
   ◊ x x   ◊ K Q x
   ♣ Q x   ♣ A x x

7. ♠ Q x x x   8. ♠ x
   ♡ J x x x   ♡ x x
   ◊ J x x x x   ◊ Q x x x
   ♣ —   ♣ J x x x x x

9. ♠ A J x x x   10. ♠ A K x x
   ♡ x x   ♡ A Q x x
   ◊ K x x   ◊ K x x
   ♣ x x x   ♣ x x

11. ♠ A Q x x x   12. ♠ A x x x
   ♡ x x   ♡ A x x x x
   ◊ x x x x   ◊ x x
   ♣ x x   ♣ J x

II. You opened 1 NT, partner responded 2 ♣, you bid 2 ◊, he said
2 ♠. What do you do now, with:

1. ♠ K x x   2. ♠ K Q x
   ♡ A Q x   ♡ A K x
   ◊ K Q x x   ◊ A x x x x
   ♣ Q x x   ♣ x x

3. ♠ K Q x   4. ♠ K x
   ♡ x x   ♡ Q J x
   ◊ A Q x x   ◊ K Q J x x
   ♣ A K x x   ♣ A x x

5. ♠ K x
   ♡ Q J x
   ◊ K Q J x
   ♣ A Q x x

III. You opened 1 NT, partner responded 2 ♣, you bid 2 ♠, he bid 2 NT. What do you do now, with:

1. ♠ K Q x x
   ♡ K x x
   ◊ A x x
   ♣ K J x

2. ♠ K Q x x
   ♡ K x x
   ◊ A Q x
   ♣ K J x

3. ♠ K Q x x
   ♡ A Q x x
   ◊ A x
   ♣ J x x

4. ♠ K Q x x
   ♡ A Q x x
   ◊ A x
   ♣ Q J x

SOLUTIONS TO STAYMAN QUIZ:

I.
1. 2 ♣
2. 2 ♣
3. Pass
4. 3 ♠   Stayman is not needed here.
5. 2 ♣   If partner says 2 ◊, jump to *3 ♠*.
6. 3 NT   Most players would avoid using Stayman on this hand because of the lack of distribution and the poor major suit.
7. 2 ♣   Plan to pass *any* bid partner makes.
8. 2 ♣   Follow up with 3 ♣, to show a bad hand with long clubs.
9. 2 ♣   Bid 2 ♠ next (unless partner responds 2 ♠ and you can raise) to show an invitational hand with five spades.
10. 2 ♣   Bid slam if you find a suit, or invite slam in notrump.
11. 2 ♠   Too weak for Stayman.
12. 2 ♣

II.
1. Pass
2. 3 ♠
3. 4 ♠
4. 2 NT
5. 3 NT

III.
1. Pass
2. 3NT
3. 3 ♡
4. 4 ♡

Chapter 3

THINKING:
INTRODUCTION TO COUNTING AS DECLARER
OPENING BIDS OF ONE OF A SUIT

THINKING: INTRODUCTION TO COUNTING AS DECLARER

We saw that declarer can sometimes locate a missing honor by *counting* the opponents' high-card points and drawing an *inference* based on what happened (or did not happen) in the bidding. Now we want to show you *another* way declarer can figure out what the opponents have. Sometimes it helps to count the *distribution* of the concealed hands. This technique takes a little persistence and practice, but it is worth the effort. Here is an example:

1.
  ♠ K Q 7 5
  ♡ 8 7 4
  ◇ A 10 6
  ♣ K 5 4

  ♠ A 10 6 3
  ♡ Q 10 5
  ◇ K J 5
  ♣ A Q 3

You opened 1 NT and reached 4♠ via the Stayman Convention. West leads the ♡A and continues with a low heart to East's king. Back comes a third heart and West ruffs your queen. Next, a trump is led. You win and draw another round, to which both opponents follow. Now the three top clubs are cashed. West follows twice and discards a diamond in the third round.

At this point, you have enough information to make your play in the diamond suit with absolute confidence! Let's examine the evidence, suit by suit.

West had *3* trumps, East had *2*.
West had *2* hearts, East had *5*.
West had *2* clubs, East had *5*.

Each opponent had 13 cards to begin with. **So how many diamonds did West have?** Six diamonds. And East had only one. Cash the ◊ K to see which diamond East had. If the queen does not appear, you can lead a diamond to dummy's ten, knowing absolutely that it will win!

It may sound complicated to remember all this information — it takes practice before you can count out an entire hand. You must realize, however, that this process is very simple *in principle*. Basically, all you do is count to 13, and anyone can do that.

Note that, in counting the opponents' distribution, you must keep track of only *one* of the concealed hands. (You can figure out the other one if you need to.) Quite often, it will be easier to count one hand than the other. For instance, if one of your opponents makes a preemptive bid, many of his cards will be known as the play *begins:*

2.
♠ A J 8 4
♡ A 7 5
◊ Q 9 5 3
♣ A 2

♠ K 10 3
♡ K 9
◊ K J 10 8 4
♣ 7 6 5

East	South	West	North
Pass	Pass	3 ♣	Double*
Pass	5 ◊	(All Pass)	

*"Takeout"

West leads the ♣K to dummy's ace. You lead a diamond to the king and West wins the ace. He cashes a club, as East shows out, and continues with a club. You ruff high in dummy and pull another round of trumps, both opponents following. **What should your next play be? Is it time to play spades now?**

Not yet. Since everything depends on the spade guess, you should postpone that play. Instead you play the ♡K, the ♡A, and a third heart, trumping. Suppose that both opponents follow to all three rounds. What do you now know about West's distribution. **How many clubs did he have?** Seven clubs. **How many diamonds?** Two. **How many hearts?** At least three. **How many spades?** *No more than one.*

33

So you have a sure thing by leading a spade to the ace and a spade to your ten.

If West had followed to only two rounds of hearts, you would know his distribution was 2-2-2-7. You would still be inclined to take the spade finesse through East, the opponent with greater length in spades. If West had showed out on the very first heart, you would know he had begun with *four* spades, so the odds would favor taking a spade finesse through *him*.

Notice how declarer should put off playing the suit in which he faces a guess until the very end of the hand, when he has the information he needs.

Let's look at one more hand:

3.
     ♠ Q 10 6 5
     ♡ A K 4 3
     ◇ K J 6
     ♣ 7 6

     ♠ A K J 8 3
     ♡ 5
     ◇ A 10 7 2
     ♣ J 8 2

You wind up in 5 ♠, West having overcalled in clubs. West cashes the ♣ A and ♣ K and continues with a third round. You ruff high in dummy and East shows out. **What was the distribution of the club suit?** West had six clubs, East had two. You draw trumps with the ace and king, and both opponents follow. So West had six clubs and two spades.

ANYONE CAN IMPROVE HIS BRIDGE BY COUNTING.

The problem is to guess the ◊ Q, of course. If you knew who had length in diamonds, you would be more inclined to play him for the missing queen. You know about spades and clubs, and you know that the opponents began with 13 cards apiece. So if you knew about the *hearts,* you could figure out the diamonds.

Play the ♡ A and ♡ K and trump a heart, digging for information. Suppose both opponents follow to three rounds of hearts. Now you know that West had six clubs, two spades, and at least three hearts. Eleven of his original 13 cards are known, so you're getting close to an answer.

Now return to dummy with a high trump and trump a fourth heart. On this trick, either both opponents will follow suit or one of them will show out. Either way, you will have a *complete count* of the hand. Say that both opponents follow to four rounds of hearts. **What was the distribution of West's hand?** West had two spades, four hearts, six clubs and . . . one diamond.

So you can make sure of your contract by leading a diamond to dummy's king and a diamond back to your ten.

OPENING ONE OF A SUIT

To open the bidding with one of a suit, you need a hand that is somewhat *better than average.* The place to draw the line is around the *13-point mark.* **Why do you suppose our system dictates an opening bid with about 13 points?** If you and your partner both pass with 13 points, you will probably *pass out* a hand on which a *game* contract is available, with your 26 points combined. A disaster! So there are very few 13 high-card-point hands that you are not willing to open. If you have as many as *14* high-card points, you *must* open (or face your partner's wrath). You may well open the bidding with slightly *fewer* than 13 high-card points if your hand contains a promising source of tricks that makes up for the lack of high cards.

Suppose you are sitting right on the 12 or 13-point fence. What are some factors that determine whether you open?

(1) Your *Quick-Trick structure.* Quick Tricks, a measure of the *defensive* worth of a hand, are counted according to the following table:

A	= 1	QT
AK in same suit	= 2	
AQ in same suit	= 1½	
KQ in same suit	= 1	
K	= ½	

If more of your points are concentrated in aces and kings, which are good defensive values, there is more incentive for you to begin the auction.

(2) The *quality of your suits* and the number of tricks they figure to produce easily.

(3) Your *spot cards.* Tens, nines, and eights are valuable cards, especially at notrump. Some experts *add a point* for possession of two tens.

(4) Your holding in the *major suits,* especially spades. If you have length in the ranking suits, you can outbid the opponents if the auction turns competitive.

(5) The ease with which you can *rebid.* When you open the bidding, you may have to bid at least once more and continue to describe your hand. A potentially uncomfortable rebid problem may influence you not to open at all.

A wide range of hands is opened with just *one* of a suit. If you open 1 ♠, you can have as few as 11 or 12 high-card points or as many as 20, or even more.

Let's look at a few hands and decide if they are worth opening:

1. ♠ Q x   Pass. This is one of those rare 13-point
    ♡ Q J x   hands that no good bridge player would
    ◊ K J x x   open. If you open hands like this, which
    ♣ K J x x   contain little defensive strength, your part-
                           ner won't be able to judge your chances

of setting the opponents if *they* start bidding. Some methods of evaluation acknowledge the lack of Quick Tricks by deducting one point for a hand with no aces. Remember the importance of your *Quick-Trick* structure in judging the true value of a hand. *Do not open any hand that is sub-minimum in high cards and contains fewer than 2 Quick Tricks.*

2. ♠ K J x x   Pass. The Quick-Trick structure is im-
   ♡ x x   proved but there are still too few prospec-
   ◊ A J x x   tive *playing tricks* to open this borderline
   ♣ K x x   hand.

3. ♠ A K x x   Open. This is only a 12-point hand, but
   ♡ x x   you have *3* Quick Tricks. Most players
   ◊ A J x x   would open this one.
   ♣ x x x

4. ♠ x   Pass. Your suits are poor, you have no
   ♡ A Q J   length in the major suits and most of your
   ◊ K J x x   points are concentrated in a short suit (a
   ♣ J x x x x   bad sign). Also, if you open 1 ♣ and part-
                   ner responds 1 ♠, as he probably will, you
are stuck for a second bid. 1 NT would suggest a balanced hand with
at least a tolerance for partner's spades; 2 ♣ is repulsive; and 2 ◊
would be particularly unsound — partner might take you back to clubs
at the *three* level, and you might be too high at a nine-trick contract.
With rebid problems looming, perhaps it is better not to open this
borderline hand.

5. ♠ A K x x x x   This is an opening bid. You have good
   ♡ A x x   defense, some tricks, and a nice suit that
   ◊ x x   will provide an easy second bid. What else
   ♣ x x   do you need to open?

Once you decide your hand is worth an opening bid, you must
pick a suit. There are some simple guidelines. First, if you have JUST
ONE SUIT longer than any other, OPEN IN IT. On the last hand
we discussed, you would clearly open 1 ♠. On this hand:

6. ♠ A K x   Open 1 ♣.
   ♡ x x
   ◊ K x
   ♣ Q J x x x x

7. ♠ A K Q   Open 1 ♣. Don't consider 1 ♠, even
   ♡ x x x   though you have honors in that suit.
   ◊ A x   *Length* is the primary consideration when
   ♣ J x x x x   you suggest a suit as trumps.

Sometimes, your "longest" suit may be only *four* cards in length.

8. ♠ x x x   Open 1 ♣, your longest suit. Quite often,
♥ A K x   *four*-card suits are bid, just as a *suggestion*
♦ A J x   about what a possible trump suit *might* be
♣ Q x x x   if partner also has length there. Remember
that, in seeking a trump suit, you desire
an *eight*-card fit or longer. A *4-4* fit will do just fine. But if no one
is willing to bid a suit of only four cards, a potential fit may be missed.
Of course, you will not bid this particular club suit a *second* time
(as you might do if you had a five or six-card suit). Nor does your
1 ♣ opening commit you to play with clubs as trumps. Partner will
not raise and agree with your suggestion unless he also has substantial club length.

What if you have more than one four-card suit to choose from?
With TWO FOUR-CARD SUITS, OPEN THE LOWER RANKING.

9. ♠ K Q x x   Open 1 ♣.
♥ x x
♦ A Q x
♣ Q J x x

10. ♠ A x   Open 1 ♦.
♥ A J x x
♦ K Q x x
♣ x x x

When your suits are only four cards long, you have no strong feelings about what trumps will be. So you prefer to start the bidding
off low to leave room to suggest other suits. On hand #9, it is likely
that partner will *respond* to your 1 ♣ opening by suggesting a *red*
suit as trumps. Now you can show your other suit by rebidding 1 ♠.
You get both of your suits suggested and you *stay low*. If you were
to open *1 ♠*, you would have to go to the *three* level to show your
clubs next if partner responded with two of a red suit.

On hand #10, partner has a convenient chance to respond in hearts
to your 1 ♦ opening (so you can expect to find a fit in either of your
suits if there is one). If he does not, you will rebid in notrump, suggesting a balanced hand.

Now let's suppose you have THREE FOUR-CARD SUITS. Finding your best strain in these situations can be awkward. The textbook

rule suggests that you open in the SUIT THAT RANKS JUST BENEATH YOUR SINGLETON. So *if* you follow this rule, you would . . .

11. ♠ Q x x x   Open 1 ♣.
    ♡ K Q x x
    ◊ x
    ♣ A K x x

12. ♠ x   Open 1 ♡.
    ♡ A Q x x
    ◊ K J x x
    ♣ A x x x

However, there are some problems with this rule. For one thing, you must open *1 ♣* with a singleton in *clubs,* which eliminates any suit responses at the one level. Most important, *ANOTHER rule takes precedence.*

Nowadays, players avoid opening in a *four-card MAJOR suit.* If the opening bid is *1 ♣*, you have lots of room to look around for your best suit. The bidding might even go: 1 ♣, 1 ◊, 1 ♡, 1 ♠, and your side could suggest every suit as trumps at the one level. So a 1 ♣ opening need not promise any particular suit quality. *Four small cards is enough.* If you open *1 ♠*, however, you have used up some bidding space. So a 1 ♠ (or 1 ♡) opening implies a better suit. You are saying, "Partner, I have a pretty good suit — we have less reason to seek another suit."

Despite the singleton in spades, nobody would open 1 ♡ with:

13. ♠ x   They would probably drop down a suit
    ♡ J x x x   and . . . open 1 ◊.
    ◊ A Q x x
    ♣ A K x x

If you combine this rule about MAJOR suit openings with the one that suggests opening in the LOWER-RANKING of two four-card suits, you will find that you almost never open a four-card MAJOR suit. In order to simplify things even more, many partnerships have agreed that THEIR MAJOR SUIT OPENINGS WILL PROMISE FIVE OR MORE CARDS. This is a strong tendency in modern bridge. The "FIVE-CARD MAJORS" style is attractive because greater accuracy in the bidding is possible when opener is known to have at least five cards in his major suit.

14. ♠ A Q x   Open 1♡. Even playing "five-card
    ♡ A K J 10   majors," you would pretend that your
    ◊ x x x   strong four-card suit was a five-carder. In
    ♣ x x x   general, however, AVOID OPENING IN
                   A FOUR-CARD MAJOR SUIT.

Remember that your partner is *anxious to raise* a MAJOR suit opening (and may do so with *three*-card support). If you open in a major
suit, picture what the contract will be like if partner raises you with
only *three* cards. Returning to a hand we discussed a minute ago:

(12.) ♠ x   Most players would prefer a 1 ◊ opening.
    ♡ A Q x x   If you tend toward "five-card majors,"
    ◊ K J x x   you will probably open 1 ◊ on most hands
    ♣ A x x x   with three four-card suits (except, of
                  course, when your singleton is in
                  diamonds).

15. ♠ Q x x x   This is an obligatory opening, but the only
    ♡ K Q x   "suit" you have is a bad four-card major.
    ◊ x x x   The least of evils is to *pretend your club*
    ♣ A K x   suit is four cards long and open in it. Part-
                  ner will be anxious to suggest another suit
or bid no-trump over your *minor*-suit opening, so nothing bad is likely
to happen.

One advantage in opening 1 ♣ with this kind of hand is that you
prepare a second bid by starting the auction off low. If partner
responds 1 ◊ or 1 ♡, you can show your spade suit next. (If you
show a major suit at your *second* turn, you promise *no* particular
suit quality.)

Since a 1 ♣ opening suggests clubs as a possible trump suit, partner may raise. If you open 1 ♣ on hand #15 above, and partner raises
to 2 ♣, *pass* and make the best of it. Partner will be careful not to
raise without adequate support. Don't panic and bid yourself into
a *hopeless* contract. (A *further* bid by you over 2 ♣ would show *interest in game,* which you *don't* have.)

40

Now say that you have *TWO LONG SUITS* with five or more cards in each. A consideration here is that *you must plan to bid both suits,* since a fit is available if partner has even as many as *three* cards in one of them. For economy's sake, it is best to begin by OPENING IN THE *HIGHER*-RANKING SUIT.* Just the opposite, you see, from your procedure with two *four*-card suits.

16.   ♠ x   Open 1 ◊ and rebid 2 ♣ over partner's
      ♡ x x   likely major-suit response. *If partner has*
      ◊ A Q x x x   *a bad hand* and wants to stop low, he can
      ♣ A K x x x   play in either of your suits *at the two level;*
                      by *passing* if he likes clubs or by taking a
preference to 2 ◊. If you open 1 ♣ and rebid 2 ◊, a 2 ♣ contract would no longer be possible.

Some authorities recommend that this rule be applied in certain situations even when your suits are only *FOUR* CARDS long.
     If you have:

17.   ♠ K Q x x   A 1 ♣ opening is clearly preferable. You
      ♡ x x   anticipate a red-suit response and you will
      ◊ A x x   be able to show your other suit easily.
      ♣ A J x x

But with:

18.   ♠ x x x   Your suits are *touching* in rank. If you
      ♡ Q x   open 1 ♣ this time, and partner responds
      ◊ A K x x   in a major suit, you will be unable to show
      ♣ A J x x   your *diamonds.* (Partner might have to
                      prefer clubs, the first suit you offered him,
and he would have to do so at the *three* level, where your side might not be safe.) The key question is whether you are *eager to show both suits,* treating your hand as a two-suiter (in which case you open with the HIGHER-RANKING suit and bid the lower-ranking next); or whether you are content to show only *one* suit and make your second bid in notrump (treating your hand as balanced). Here we suggest a 1 ♣ opening.

———
*Many players make an exception and open 1 ♣ on certain hands with five clubs and five spades.

As we said, some authorities suggest that you open the HIGHER-RANKING of two FOUR-CARD SUITS THAT ARE *TOUCHING IN RANK*. Remember, however, that if you open 1 ◇ on:

(10). ♠ A x   *Partner* will have a convenient chance to
      ♡ A J x x   suggest the hearts. We think that, unless
      ◇ K Q x x   you have two *exceptionally strong* four-
      ♣ x x x   card suits and you are willing to treat them
as if they were *long* suits, you should open
in the LOWER-RANKNG of two FOUR-CARD SUITS, no matter
what your suits are. In any case, avoid opening in a four-card major
suit.

19. ♠ A x   Open 1 ♡. Unless your hand is very
    ♡ K Q 10 x x   strong in high cards, you should be con-
    ◇ Q J 10 x x x   cerned with *economy*. This is a rare ex-
    ♣ —   ception to the general rule of opening in
                           your *longest* suit.

20. ♠ K x   Open 1 NT. A five-card suit (even a *major*
    ♡ A Q x x x   suit) is no bar to opening 1 NT if your
    ◇ K J x   hand is suitable.
    ♣ A 10 x

21. ♠ A Q x x   Open 1 ◇. You are too strong to open
    ♡ Q x   1 NT, so you open in the lower-ranking
    ◇ A K x x   four-card suit. Partner will respond if he
    ♣ A x x   has a little strength and you can bid
                      strongly at your next turn.

Let's review the guidelines we have learned in choosing an opening bid:

WITH ONE LONG SUIT — open one of that suit. (Minor suits only four cards long are often opened.)

WITH TWO LONG SUITS (five cards or more in each one) — usually open the higher-ranking suit. (With five clubs and five spades, usually open 1♣.)

WITH TWO FOUR-CARD MINOR SUITS — open 1♣.*

NOTE WELL: WITH ONE FOUR-CARD MINOR SUIT and no longer suit, open in the minor. AVOID OPENING IN A FOUR-CARD MAJOR SUIT (unless your suit is so strong that you would welcome a raise with only three cards).

Since most players promise at least a five-card suit when they open in a major suit, you are often obliged to open a good three-card minor suit (clubs, unless your distribution is precisely 4-4-3-2). The alternative, opening a four-card major, is worse. Many players call this bid the "short club," but "prepared bid" is more accurate. One advantage of this opening is that it starts the auction low and allows you to keep another suit in reserve for a rebid.

---

*If balanced, you plan to rebid in notrump. However, with very strong diamonds, or with two four-card minors so strong that you will treat your hand as a two-suiter and show both suits, a 1♦ opening is preferable.

Also, some hands with *three* four-card suits require special treatment. If you have 1-4-4-4 distribution, a 1♠ response to 1♣ would leave you without a good rebid; with 4-1-4-4 distribution, a 1 NT response to a 1♣ opening would be awkward. In both cases, therefore, tend to open 1♦.

For further explanation, see the material on opener's rebid, especially the discussion of reverses.

43

TEST YOUR COMPREHENSION OF THE MATERIAL IN THIS CHAPTER:

QUIZ ON COUNTING AS DECLARER:

1.
        ♠ Q 9 5 3
        ♡ Q 7 5
        ◇ K 10 6 4
        ♣ K 5

        ♠ A K 10 6 2
        ♡ 8
        ◇ A J 3
        ♣ A Q 6 2

    You are declarer in 6♠ after East overcalled in hearts. The opening lead is the ♡J, and you ruff the second heart. You draw trumps, finding that East had three. Next you play the three top clubs and ruff your fourth club in dummy. East follows suit to all four rounds, and West discards a diamond on the fourth club. What is East's distribution? How do you play the diamond suit?

2.
        ♠ K 10 7 2
        ♡ Q 7 5
        ◇ A K 3
        ♣ A 9 4

        ♠ A Q 9 6 4 3
        ♡ 4
        ◇ 8 6
        ♣ K 10 7 3

    After East opened 3♡, you and partner got overboard in 6♠. West leads the ♡A and another heart and you ruff. You draw two rounds of trumps, finding East with two. Next you play the high diamonds and ruff a diamond. Both opponents follow suit. A trump to dummy is followed by a heart ruff, and West discards a diamond. What is East's probable distribution? How do you play the clubs?

3.

        ♠ 7 6 5
        ♡ A Q 4
        ◊ 8 7 4 3
        ♣ K J 6

        ♠ K Q J
        ♡ K 7 2
        ◊ A K Q J
        ♣ A 10 4

West leads the ♠ 10 against your 6 NT contract. East wins the ace and returns a spade. When you cash the other high spade, East discards a club. Both opponents follow suit to the three top hearts. You cash the diamonds next, and West follows to four rounds, while East discards the 13th heart and two more clubs. What is West's distribution? What is East's distribution? How do you play the club suit?

SOLUTIONS:

1.   East showed up with three spades and four clubs, and should have five or more hearts for his overcall. So he had at most one diamond. Cash the ◊ A and lead a diamond to the 10.
2.   East had two spades, seven hearts, and at least three diamonds. So he had one club at most. Your only chance is that East had a singleton club *honor*. Cash the ♣ K, and if an honor appears to your right, lead a club to dummy's 9.
3.   West had five spades, three hearts, four diamonds, and one club. East had two spades, four hearts, one diamond, and six clubs. Lead a club to the king and a club to your 10.

QUIZ ON OPENING ONE OF A SUIT:

Decide whether each of these hands is an opening bid and, if so, in what suit you should open.

1. ♠ K x
     ♡ Q J x x
     ◊ K J x x
     ♣ Q J x

2. ♠ K
     ♡ A J x
     ◊ K x x x
     ♣ J x x x x

3.   ♠ A Q x x x x
     ♡ A J x
     ◇ x x
     ♣ x x

4.   ♠ A x x x
     ♡ Q x x
     ◇ Q x x
     ♣ A x x

5.   ♠ A K x x
     ♡ x x
     ◇ x x x
     ♣ A J x x

6.   ♠ A 10 9 x
     ♡ x x
     ◇ A J 10 x
     ♣ K 10 x

7.   ♠ A J 10 x x
     ♡ A J 10 x x
     ◇ Q x
     ♣ x

8.   ♠ A J x x x x x
     ♡ A J x x
     ◇ x
     ♣ x

9.   ♠ A
     ♡ Q x
     ◇ Q x x x x
     ♣ K x x x x

10.   ♠ A Q 10 x
     ♡ x x x
     ◇ A Q x x
     ♣ x x

11.   ♠ A K Q x x x
     ♡ K x
     ◇ x x
     ♣ x x x

12.   ♠ A K
     ♡ K x
     ◇ x x x
     ♣ Q J x x x x

13.   ♠ A K x
     ♡ K x x
     ◇ x x x
     ♣ Q J x x

14.   ♠ A K x
     ♡ x x x
     ◇ A Q x
     ♣ J x x x

15.   ♠ A K x
     ♡ x x x
     ◇ J x x x
     ♣ A Q x

16.   ♠ J x x x x
     ♡ A K x x
     ◇ A Q x
     ♣ x

17.   ♠ A K Q
     ♡ J x x x x
     ◇ —
     ♣ K x x x x

18.   ♠ A K x x
     ♡ x x x
     ◇ J x
     ♣ A J x x

19. ♠ A x
    ♡ K Q x x
    ◊ A J x x
    ♣ x x x

20. ♠ x x
    ♡ A x x
    ◊ A Q x x
    ♣ K J x x

21. ♠ x x
    ♡ A K x x
    ◊ Q x x
    ♣ K J x x

22. ♠ x x
    ♡ A K J x
    ◊ J x x
    ♣ Q J x x

23. ♠ K J x x
    ♡ A x x x
    ◊ x
    ♣ A J x x

24. ♠ K J x x
    ♡ x
    ◊ A J x x
    ♣ K Q x x

25. ♠ J x x x
    ♡ A J x x
    ◊ A K x x
    ♣ x

26. ♠ A J x x
    ♡ x
    ◊ x x x x
    ♣ A K J 10

27. ♠ x x
    ♡ x x x
    ◊ A K J x
    ♣ A K J 10

28. ♠ A x x x
    ♡ x x x
    ◊ K x x
    ♣ A Q x

29. ♠ K x x x
    ♡ Q x x x
    ◊ J x
    ♣ A K x

30. ♠ J x x x
    ♡ Q x x x
    ◊ A K x
    ♣ A x

31. ♠ A Q x
    ♡ A K J 10
    ◊ x x x
    ♣ x x x

32. ♠ A J x x x
    ♡ A K x x x
    ◊ x x
    ♣ x

33. ♠ x
    ♡ A Q x x x
    ◊ K x
    ♣ A J x x x

34. ♠ Q x
    ♡ A Q x x x
    ◊ K J x
    ♣ A 10 x

35. ♠ A K x x
    ♡ x x
    ◇ A K Q x
    ♣ K x x

36. ♠ A K J x x
    ♡ K Q x x
    ◇ x
    ♣ A J x

37. ♠ x
    ♡ A K x x
    ◇ A Q J x
    ♣ A Q x x

38. ♠ Q x x x x
    ♡ A x
    ◇ x
    ♣ A Q J x x

39. ♠ A x
    ♡ K Q x x x
    ◇ Q J x x x x
    ♣ —

40. ♠ A Q x x x
    ♡ A K J x x
    ◇ A x
    ♣ x

SOLUTIONS:

1. Pass; lacking in defensive strength.
2. Pass; bad suits, poor defense, rebid problems.
3. 1♠.
4. Pass; too many losers.
5. 1♣.
6. 1◇; good spot cards.
7. 1♠.
8. 1♠; winners, defensive tricks, an easy second bid.
9. Pass; bad suits.
10. 1◇; 3 Quick Tricks.
11. 1♠.
12. 1♣.
13. 1♣.
14. 1♣.
15. 1◇.
16. 1♠.
17. 1♡.
18. 1♣.
19. 1◇.
20. 1♣.
21. 1♣.
22. Pass; this is a borderline hand — an opening bid of 1♣ certainly could not be criticized.
23. 1♣.
24. 1◇.

25. 1 ◊.
26. 1 ♣. Diamonds are weak, clubs are very strong.
27. 1 ◊ ; treating this hand as a two-suiter and planning to bid both suits.
28. 1 ♣.
29. 1 ♣.
30. 1 ◊.
31. 1 ♡.
32. 1 ♠.
33. 1 ♡.
34. 1 NT; this is a balanced 16-count.
35. 1 ◊.
36. 1 ♠.
37. 1 ◊ ; some very strong hands must be opened with a bid of just *one* of a suit.
38. 1 ♣; an exception to our rule of handling two long suits.
39. 1 ♡; another exceptional case; with this minimum hand, you should be interested in *economy*.
40. 1 ♠; don't make the mistake of opening 1 ♡, planning to "reverse" into spades. Open 1 ♠, *jump in hearts*.

KNOWING THE CORRECT OPENING BID IS
SWEET MUSIC TO YOUR PARTNER'S EARS.

Chapter 4

THINKING: WHEN TO DRAW TRUMPS
RESPONSES TO OPENING BIDS

THINKING: WHEN TO DRAW TRUMPS

We continue our discussion of how a good declarer's thought processes work. So far, we have learned how declarer can use *counting* and *drawing inferences* to help him. Perhaps we should look more closely at some basic *technique* that every declarer should know.

Drawing the opponents' trumps is an important step in declaring many suit contracts. Declarer will usually have many more trumps than the defending side. Clearly, it will be foolish for him to leave trumps outstanding (and risk having some of his good tricks ruffed by the defense) when he can easily draw them. However, players are inclined to draw trumps first and think about it later. They fail to consider the play of the entire hand and what problems may arise. Often, drawing trumps *must* be delayed or omitted entirely.

> DRAW TRUMPS IMMEDIATELY *ONLY* IF THE HAND APPEARS TO PRESENT *NO PROBLEMS* WHATEVER. IF YOU CAN SEE A REASON NOT TO DRAW TRUMPS IMMEDIATELY, *WAIT* UNTIL THE PROPER TIME.

WHEN YOU ARE DECLARER, IT IS IMPORTANT TO KNOW WHEN TO DRAW TRUMPS AND WHEN TO WAIT.

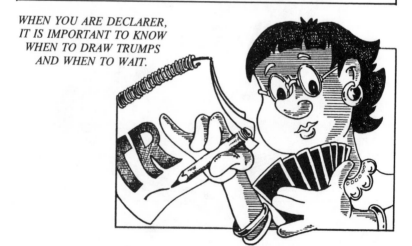

Let's list some times when you may want to delay drawing trumps:

---

1. When you need to *ruff* losers with the trumps in dummy.
2. When you are ruffing cards in your own hand in playing a *dummy reversal.*
3. When playing a *cross-ruff.* You will *never* draw trumps in this type of play.
4. When you need *entries* that only the trump suit can provide.
5. When you have *something more important to do* first, like establishing a discard for an impending loser.
6. When *keeping control* of the play dictates that you establish a side suit first.
7. When the opponents remain with *a high trump* that they will get inevitably. You may wish to go about your business of establishing and/or cashing your other tricks, ignoring the opponents' sure trump trick. (We will, however, see a hand in which you must go against this idea.)

By contrast, the time when you *do* want to draw trumps is when you have plenty of winners, no problems, everything under control. Look at this hand, for example:

1.
      ♠ K 10 5 4
      ♡ A Q 10 3
      ◊ 4 3 2
      ♣ 8 4

      ♠ A Q J 8 6
      ♡ J 4
      ◊ 9 6
      ♣ A K 7 6

Declarer has reached a 4♠ contract. The opponents lead high diamonds and declarer ruffs the third one. He draws trumps in three rounds and takes the heart finesse. If it works he discards one of his small clubs and ruffs the other one in dummy, making five. An easier hand could hardly be imagined, and that is why declarer's first play was to draw trumps.

51

Now let's look at some hands in which declarer *must decide whether to draw trumps right away.*

2.
    ♠ 4 3 2
    ♡ 4 3
    ◇ A K 4 3 2
    ♣ Q 4 3

    ♠ A K 8 7 6
    ♡ K Q J 10
    ◇ Q 7 6
    ♣ 2

The ♣J is led against declarer's 4♠ contract. He ruffs the second club and leads the ♡K, since there are a few potential pitfalls in the play. The opponents win their ♡A and force declarer to ruff another club. With plenty of good tricks available, declarer now leads his ♠A and ♠K. Both opponents follow and one high trump is still out. **Should declarer lead a third round of trumps and dislodge the last trump?** No, of course not. If declarer leads another trump there will be no more trumps in either his hand or dummy. The opponents will be in control with the lead and good clubs to cash. Instead, declarer begins to play his red-suit winners, letting the opponents ruff in with their good trump whenever they want to. Declarer still has a trump left (in either hand) to regain the lead. This technique of LEAVING THE MASTER TRUMP AT LARGE is a common way declarer can gain time in the play.

3.
    ♠ K 4 3 2
    ♡ 3 2
    ◇ 4 3 2
    ♣ K Q J 3

    ♠ 6 5
    ♡ A K 8 7 6 5
    ◇ A Q 5
    ♣ A 7

Declarer is in 4♡, and the opening lead is the ♠Q. Dummy ducks and spades are continued, declarer ruffing the third round. Both opponents follow to the ace and king of trumps. **Should declarer lead a third round of trumps in this situation?** *Yes,* he should, because he has all suits under control and plenty of winners. If declarer were to abandon trumps and begin running his club tricks, somebody might ruff in before declarer had taken all his discards, leaving him stranded with a diamond loser. If declarer concedes the high trump *here,* he assures that his run of the clubs will not be interrupted.

4. ♠ K Q 10 2
    ♡ 3
    ◊ A 6 5 4 3
    ♣ K Q 3

    ♠ A J 9 4
    ♡ A 6 5 4 2
    ◊ 8
    ♣ A 7 6

Suppose you are declarer in a contract of 7♠. (It is unlikely that anyone would actually reach a grand slam. Let's say you have been kibitzing a couple of madmen who bid as if there were no tomorrow, and one of them has to leave and asks you to play this hand for him.) The opening lead is the ◊ K. **How do you play?** Your best chance is to cross-ruff the entire hand. You hope to make all eight of your trumps separately, plus the three top clubs and the two red aces.

In a cross-ruff, you will never be able to draw trumps, so your side winners must be cashed quickly. Toward the *end* of the hand, the opponents will have nothing but trumps left and will be able to ruff your winners. So cash your high clubs, hoping nobody ruffs, and then start cross-ruffing. Note that your trumps are high enough to prevent any overruffs.

5. ♠ K Q 2
    ♡ 5 4 3
    ◊ 4 3
    ♣ A K 5 4 3

    ♠ A J 10 9 7 3
    ♡ A 8 7
    ◊ K 5
    ♣ 8 7

Declarer plays 4♠ and the ♡ Q is led. There are nine top tricks and the tenth trick can come from either a successful finesse of the

◇ K or a long card in clubs. If declarer wants to set up clubs, he will need entries to dummy, so the trumps cannot be touched for now. Instead, declarer plays the top clubs and ruffs a club (high). If the suit splits evenly, declarer can draw three rounds of trumps ending in dummy, then take his club winners, discarding hearts.

Suppose clubs break 4-2, the most likely division. After ruffing the third club, declarer returns to dummy with a trump and ruffs a fourth club (high). Now the fifth club will be good for a trick. Declarer can draw two more trumps, ending in dummy, and pitch a heart on the long club. He can now lead up to his ◇ K and may even make an overtrick.

So the trump suit may provide declarer with *transportation*. He may need entries to set up a suit or to take finesses.

6.   ♠ A 5 4
      ♡ Q 5 4
      ◇ K Q 6
      ♣ J 9 5 4

      ♠ K 8 7
      ♡ A K 7
      ◇ 4
      ♣ K Q 10 7 3 2

One common reason for waiting to draw trumps is that there may be *more pressing matters*. On this hand, the contract is 5 ♣, and the opponents lead the ♠ Q. Declarer has two aces to lose and there is also a spade loser. Declarer's plan should be to establish a diamond trick and discard his losing spade. *But he must set up his diamond trick right away.* If he leads a trump first, the opponents will lead spades again, setting up their winner in that suit before declarer has established his discard. Declarer will have "lost a tempo," as we say. The correct play by declarer is a diamond at trick two.

7.   ♠ A J 2
      ♡ K 4
      ◇ 7 6 5 4
      ♣ 5 4 3 2

      ♠ 3
      ♡ A Q J 10 9 5
      ◇ A K
      ♣ 10 9 7 6

The ♠ 10 is led against your 4 ♡ contract, and dummy wins the ace. **How do you plan the play?** You have nine easy tricks. The tenth will have to be established in clubs, assuming there is a 3-2 split. **At what point will you draw trumps?** The problem here is one of *control* if the trumps split *4-1* against you. Suppose you draw trumps early and find that 4-1 break. You will have *two* trumps left and must give the opponents the lead with clubs *three* times before you get a club trick set up. They will lead spades at every opportunity and force you to *lose control*.

Remember our basic idea about drawing trumps. If there is any potential problem, it may be wise to *delay*. Here, you must start on *clubs* right away. The opponents can force you to ruff spades the first two times they win a club trick. But after you concede the third club (still having drawn no trumps), the *dummy* will be out of spades and can ruff any further spade leads, allowing you to *preserve four trumps* in your own hand and keep control.

RESPONDING TO SUIT OPENINGS

When the opening bid is 1 NT, responder can answer the two key questions about *STRENGTH* and *FIT* right away, since opener's hand is so well-defined. Auctions that begin with a bid of one of a suit can be more complicated, however. Responder cannot place the contract immediately because opener's bid can cover a *wide range* of possible hands. It may take several bids before the partnership can exchange enough information to place the contract.

Let's review some of the ways responder can keep the conversation going at his first turn:

WITH A *RAISE* OF OPENER'S SUIT to two, three, or straight to game. A RAISE is a desirable action, especially if partner's suit is a major, because you confirm a trump suit immediately and tell partner about how much strength you hold.

WITH A BID OF A *NEW SUIT*. This is an attractive option since finding the best available trump suit, particularly if it is a *major* suit, is important.

WITH A RESPONSE IN *NOTRUMP*, if neither of the first two options is available.

Let's drill on these responses and their meanings. Partner has opened 1♡. Give the proper response with these hands.

1. ♠ J x x x   Pass. You do *not* respond with fewer than
    ♡ x   6 points.
    ◊ Q x x x x x
    ♣ x x

2. ♠ x x   2♡. A *single raise* shows 6-9 points and
    ♡ Q x x x   support for partner's suit. (Four-card sup-
    ◊ A J x x x   port is desired, but you may raise a *major*
    ♣ x x   suit opening to *two* with only three cards.)
                      There is no reason to bid diamonds here
because you *know* hearts will be a good trump suit.

3. ♠ x x   3♡. A *double raise* shows 13-15 points,
    ♡ K J x x   good support (four cards or more no
    ◊ A Q x x   matter what suit partner opened), and is
    ♣ K x x   *forcing.*

4. ♠ x   4♡. A *leap to game* shows a huge fit for
    ♡ K J x x x   partner's suit, a distributional hand, but
    ◊ Q J x x x   fewer than 10 high-card points. The bid
    ♣ x x   is primarily *preemptive.*

5. ♠ K J x x   1♠. Responder may suggest a *new suit*
    ♡ x   at the one level with as few as 6 points.
    ◊ Q x x x   *Any* suit of four cards or more may be
    ♣ x x x x   suggested.

6. ♠ A Q x x x   1♠. Responder may choose to suggest a
    ♡ x   suit cheaply even if he intends to bid a lot
    ◊ K J x x   more. This save space so the partnership
    ♣ K J x   can exchange information before the bid-
                      ding gets too high. It's safe to bid only
1♠ because a *NEW SUIT BY RESPONDER IS A FORCING BID.*

7. ♠ A x x   2♣. If responder must go to the *two* level
    ♡ x x   to show his suit, he needs 10 high-card
    ◊ K x x   points or more.
    ♣ K J x x x

8. ♠ A x x   1 NT. This response shows 6-9 points,
   ♡ x x   denies support for partner's suit, and
   ◊ x x x   denies a suit that responder could suggest
   ♣ K J x x x   at the one level. Sometimes this response
                      must be made on an *unbalanced* hand.

9. ♠ A 10 x   2 NT. This shows 13-15 points, a
   ♡ J x x   balanced hand, and stoppers in all the
   ◊ K Q x x   unbid suits (and possibly opener's suit as
   ♣ K J x   well). Another *forcing* response.

10. ♠ A 10 x   3 NT. This shows 16-18 points and a
    ♡ K x x   balanced hand, an easy response to re-
    ◊ K Q x x   member since you would have opened
    ♣ K J x   1 NT as dealer. This response is *not* forc-
                     ing. Since game has been reached, opener
                     may pass.

11. ♠ A K Q J x x   2♠. A *jump shift* by responder suggests
    ♡ Q x   interest in slam. Remember that *any* new-
    ◊ A x x   suit bid is forcing, so you *do not have to*
    ♣ x x   jump just to show *game* interest.

Suppose we look at some problem situations responder may have at his first turn. The opening bid is still 1 ♡.

12. ♠ K x x x   1♠. You would like to suggest your
    ♡ x x   better suit as trumps, but you lack the
    ◊ K Q x x x   high-card strength to respond at the *two*
    ♣ x x   level.

13. ♠ x x x   2♣. No immediate heart raise is appro-
    ♡ Q x x x   priate. You must *temporize* (your new-suit
    ◊ A x x   response at the two level shows 10 points
    ♣ K Q x   or more, remember), and support hearts
                     at your next turn. There is no harm here
in bidding a non-suit, since you can always return to hearts (a higher-ranking suit) if partner keeps raising clubs.

14. ♠ Q x x x   1♠. Do not make the mistake of respond-
     ♡ x x   ing 1 NT to show your point-count. Look
     ◊ K x x   for a suit if you can. Partner can always
     ♣ K x x x   suggest notrump if he has no support for
                    spades.

15. ♠ A K x x   Here you plan to do a lot of bidding, so
     ♡ x x   you can show your suits in their natural
     ◊ Q x   order. Respond 2♣, planning to bid 2♠
     ♣ A Q x x x   over partner's likely 2♡ rebid. If your
                    hand were worth only one response, you
                    might show your major suit.

16. ♠ A J x x x   2♡ is the best response. You can *raise*
     ♡ Q x x   *in the known fit* and show your point
     ◊ x x   count at the same time.
     ♣ x x x

17. ♠ A x x   2♡. Nowadays, when a *major* suit open-
     ♡ x x x   ing is based on *five* or more cards, most
     ◊ A x   players cheerfully raise (to two) with *any*
     ♣ x x x x x   three-card support.

In the remainder of the problems, the opening bid is *1♣*.

18. ♠ A x x   2♣. Don't be afraid to raise. If partner
     ♡ x x   has opened with a *prepared bid*, that is
     ◊ x x x x   his business.
     ♣ K J x x

19. ♠ x x   1◊. You must *temporize*, lacking a suit-
     ♡ K x x   able club raise at your first turn.
     ◊ A x x x
     ♣ K J x x

20. ♠ Q x x x x   1♠. Show your *longest* suit.
     ♡ A Q x x
     ◊ J x
     ♣ x x

21. ♠ K x x x   With two four-card majors to suggest,
    ♡ Q x x x   show them "up-the-line." Partner can
    ◇ A x   raise your 1 ♡ response with support; or,
    ♣ x x x   if he has a four-card spade suit, he can
                       continue with 1 ♠ and you can raise him.
A fit in either suit is found with no problem. It's the same principle
you apply when choosing an opening bid with two four-card suits.

22. ♠ A J x x x   Respond 1 ♠. With two *long* suits, both of
    ♡ K J x x x   which you must plan to bid *yourself,* you
    ◇ x x   respond in the *higher*-ranking suit to begin
    ♣ x   with.

23. ♠ x x   Most players would respond 1 ♡ and let
    ♡ K x x x   the club support go, at least temporarily.
    ◇ x x x   You will *seldom suppress* a major suit be-
    ♣ A Q x x   cause finding a fit in a *major* is so
                       important.

24. ♠ A Q x   1 ♡. First you look for a fit in the major
    ♡ K Q x x   suit. Later you will show the *strength* of
    ◇ x x x   your hand.
    ♣ K x x

25. ♠ A Q x   2 NT. 1 ◇ is acceptable, but finding a fit
    ♡ K J x   in diamonds is relatively unimportant,
    ◇ K 10 x x   especially when your hand looks so good
    ♣ x x x   for notrump.

26. ♠ x x   2 ♡. You plan to support clubs next, sug-
    ♡ A K J x x   gesting that your slam interest is based on
    ◇ A x   an excellent fit for partner's suit. Note
    ♣ K Q x x   that, *when you jump shift, you have a
                       good idea in what strain* the contract will
be played, so that you are willing to *use up* a level of bidding that
might be needed to look for a suit.

27. ♠ A Q x x   1 ◇ (or 1 ♡). It is wrong to jump shift on
    ♡ A K J x   this hand, even though it contains more
    ◇ K Q x x   high-card points than #26, because you
    ♣ x   are not sure what suit, if any, will be
                       trumps. You need bidding space to look
                       for your best strain.

59

28. ♠ —
    ♡ Q x x
    ◊ x x x x
    ♣ Q J x x x x

4♣. This bid is *preemptive,* made to keep the opponents from getting into the auction easily.

29. ♠ K Q J x x x x
    ♡ x
    ◊ J x x
    ♣ x x

3♠. You still have preemptive bids available even after *partner* opens the bidding. In considering any preemptive action, the *vulnerability is a factor,* however.

RESPONDING TO THE OPENING BID: REVIEW

With 6 points or more, RESPOND if partner opens the bidding with one of a suit. You should respond, even with a poorish hand, because partner could have *20+* for his opening, and game is still possible. Also, the suit partner suggests as trumps with his first bid may not be the best one available to your side. You may wish to suggest another suit. You are especially interested in finding a *major* suit for trumps.

While you may be obliged to respond with weakness, you may also choose to respond with a *minimum* bid even if your hand is fairly *strong.* You save bidding room so you and partner can exchange as much information as possible.

BRIDGE IS AN EASY GAME WHEN YOU BID WELL!

Responder has several options at his first turn. They fall into three categories:

RAISE partner's suit to two with 6-9 points and four-card support. (It is permissible to raise a *major*-suit opening to *two* with only *three*-card support.)

RAISE partner's suit to three with 13-15 points and good four-card support or better. This is *forcing*. Partner must continue at least to game.

RAISE partner's suit straight to game with excellent support and a distributional hand, but fewer than 10 high-card points. This bid is primarily preemptive, intended to keep the opponents from bidding.

BID A NEW SUIT at the one level with 6 points or more.

BID A NEW SUIT at the two level with 10 points or more. Responder may bid *any* suit* of four or more cards, just as a suggestion about a suit that *could* be trumps. Any new-suit bid by responder is *forcing,* and you may choose to respond as cheaply as possible even with a sound hand in order to conserve bidding space. Therefore . . .

JUMP IN A NEW SUIT only with a good suit and a very powerful hand. Responder can thus alert his partner that a slam contract is a strong possibility.

BID 1 NT with 6-9 points, no support for your partner's suit, and no suit of your own that you could show at the one level.

BID 2 NT with 13-15 points, balanced pattern, and a "stopper" in all the unbid suits. This bid is *forcing*.

BID 3 NT with 16-18 points and balanced pattern.

Rarely, responder may choose a *preemptive* response. If the opening bid, for example, is 1 ◇, responses of *4* ◇ or *three of a major suit* would be *preemptive*.

---

*The only exception is that a 2 ♡ response to a 1 ♠ opening suggests five or more hearts.

TEST YOUR COMPREHENSION OF THE MATERIAL IN THIS CHAPTER:

QUIZ ON DRAWING TRUMPS:

1. ♠ A K
    ♡ A Q J 10
    ◊ 4 3 2
    ♣ Q 10 8 7

    ♠ 4 3
    ♡ 5 4 3
    ◊ K 7 6
    ♣ A K J 3 2

    Contract: 5 ♣
    Opening lead: ♠ Q
    Plan the play.

2. ♠ Q J
    ♡ J 9 4 2
    ◊ A 4 3
    ♣ 6 5 4 3

    ♠ A 10 5
    ♡ A Q 10 6 5
    ◊ K 6 5
    ♣ K Q

    Contract: 4 ♡
    Opening lead: ◊ Q
    Plan the play.

3. ♠ 3 2
    ♡ A K Q J 10
    ◊ 2
    ♣ A 7 6 5 4

    ♠ A K 8 7 6 5
    ♡ 3 2
    ◊ A 8 7 6
    ♣ 8

    Contract: 6 ♠
    Opening lead: ◊ K
    Plan the play.

4. ♠ J 5
    ♡ Q 7 6 5 4
    ◊ Q 10 4 3
    ♣ Q 3

    ♠ A K Q 10 9 4
    ♡ K 2
    ◊ K J 7 5
    ♣ J

    Contract: 4 ♠
    Opening lead: ♣ 2
    The ace wins to
    your right and a
    club is returned.
    Plan the play.

SOLUTIONS:

1. Declarer may need to finesse in hearts *three* times so he must be careful with his entries to hand. He plays a trump to the jack and finesses in hearts; then queen of trumps and a trump to the ace, another heart finesse; finally, a trump to the king for another heart finesse, if necessary.

2. Declarer has a potential loser in each suit, but he can *discard a diamond from dummy on a spade*. He should win the opening lead in dummy and make a spade play *immediately,* setting up his pitch. If he takes a (losing) trump finesse at trick two, the defenders will get to lead diamonds again, setting up their winner, and declarer will have "lost a tempo" and maybe his contract.

3. Declarer's best play is to win the ◊ A and *duck a round of trumps*. He can win whatever the opponents lead next, draw two more rounds of trumps (hopefully all of them) and run his winners without fear the opponents will ruff in. There are potential problems on any other line of play.

4. If declarer ruffs the second club and draws trumps, he will be in trouble if trumps split 4-1. He will have only *one* trump left and must knock out *two* aces to come to ten tricks. The opponents will lead clubs at every opportunity and declarer will *lose control*. Declarer should instead lead *a low heart at trick two*. If he wins this trick, he can draw trumps (even if they are 4-1) and knock out the ◊ A for ten tricks. Even if the opponents win the first heart, they cannot force declarer in clubs because dummy is *also* void and still has some trumps. (It is true that declarer might run into a diamond ruff if he does not draw trumps right away; but the opponents did not try for a diamond ruff when they had the chance. A 4-1 trump break is a bigger danger.)

QUIZ ON RESPONDING TO SUIT OPENINGS:

I. Partner has opened 1♠. Give the correct response with:

1. ♠ J x x
    ♡ Q x
    ◊ Q x x x
    ♣ x x x x

2. ♠ J x x x
    ♡ x x
    ◊ A Q x x
    ♣ x x x

3. ♠ J x x
    ♡ x x
    ◊ A Q x x x
    ♣ x x x

4. ♠ A K x x
    ♡ x x
    ◊ A x x x
    ♣ Q x x

5. ♠ Q J x x x
    ♡ —
    ◊ Q 10 x x x x
    ♣ x x

6. ♠ x x
    ♡ K Q x x x
    ◊ x x x
    ♣ K x x

7. ♠ x
    ♡ K x x
    ◊ x x x
    ♣ K J x x x x

8. ♠ x x
    ♡ A J x x
    ◊ K Q x
    ♣ K J x x

9. ♠ Q x
    ♡ K x x
    ◊ A Q x x
    ♣ A J x x

10. ♠ x x
    ♡ A K x
    ◊ x x x
    ♣ K J x x x

11. ♠ A K x x
    ♡ x
    ◊ A x x
    ♣ K Q 10 x x

12. ♠ x
    ♡ A Q x x
    ◊ A K x
    ♣ K Q x x x

13. ♠ x
    ♡ K x x x
    ◊ A Q x x
    ♣ A x x x

14. ♠ Q x x x
    ♡ x x
    ◊ A K J x
    ♣ x x x

15. ♠ A Q x x
    ♡ x x
    ◊ A K J 10 x
    ♣ x x

II. Partner has opened 1 ◊ . Give the correct response with:

1. ♠ x x
   ♡ A K
   ◊ J x x x x
   ♣ x x x x

2. ♠ x x
   ♡ A x x
   ◊ A Q x x x
   ♣ K x x

3. ♠ K J x x
   ♡ Q x x
   ◊ x x x
   ♣ x x x

4. ♠ A K x x x
   ♡ A x x
   ◊ K x x
   ♣ x x

5. ♠ A J x x
   ♡ Q x x x
   ◊ x x
   ♣ J x x

6. ♠ A x x x x
   ♡ Q J x x x
   ◊ x
   ♣ A x

7. ♠ A K Q 10
   ♡ K Q 10 x
   ◊ x x
   ♣ x x x

8. ♠ Q x x
   ♡ K x x
   ◊ A x x
   ♣ x x x x

9. ♠ K J x
   ♡ A 10 x
   ◊ J x x
   ♣ K Q x x

10. ♠ K J x
    ♡ A 10 x
    ◊ J x x x
    ♣ K Q x

11. ♠ A Q x
    ♡ K Q x
    ◊ J x x
    ♣ K Q x x

12. ♠ K J x
    ♡ A Q x x
    ◊ x x
    ♣ K x x x

13. ♠ A K J x x
    ♡ A x
    ◊ A J x x
    ♣ x x

14. ♠ A Q x x
    ♡ A K x x
    ◊ x
    ♣ A J x x

15. ♠ —
    ♡ x x x
    ◊ K Q 10 x x x
    ♣ J 10 x x

III. With each of these hands, give the correct response to an opening bid in each of the four suits:

1. ♠ x
   ♡ K 10 x x x x
   ◊ Q J x
   ♣ J x x

2. ♠ x x
   ♡ A J x x
   ◊ K Q x x
   ♣ K 10 x

3. ♠ x x
   ♡ A Q x x
   ◊ x x x
   ♣ A K x x

4. ♠ A x
   ♡ K x x x
   ◊ x x x
   ♣ K J x x

5. ♠ A K
   ♡ J x x x
   ◊ 10 x x x
   ♣ x x x

SOLUTIONS:

I. 1. Pass
    2. 2 ♠
    3. 2 ♠
    4. 3 ♠
    5. 4 ♠
    6. 1 NT
    7. 1 NT   (no choice)
    8. 2 NT
    9. 3 NT
   10. 2 ♣
   11. 3 ♣   (planning to support spades next)
   12. 2 ♣   (save room to find your best strain)
   13. 2 ♣   (avoid a 2 NT response with unbalanced pattern)
   14. 2 ◊   (you must temporize)
   15. 2 ◊   (you may show a *very strong side* suit even when a double raise of partner's suit is possible)

66

II. 1. 2♢
    2. 3♢
    3. 1♠
    4. 1♠
    5. 1♡   (show four-card majors "up-the-line.")
    6. 1♠
    7. 1♠   (an exception; since these suits are so strong, you
             should treat them as long suits and plan to bid both
             of them.)
    8. 1 NT
    9. 2 NT
   10. 2 NT (more descriptive than a diamond raise)
   11. 3 NT
   12. 1♡
   13. 2♠
   14. 1♡   (save room because the best trump suit is in
             doubt.)
   15. 4♢   (but the vulnerability must be considered before
             making this bid)

III. 1. 1♠ - 1 NT   2. 1♠ - 2 NT
         1♡ - 4♡   1♡ - 3♡
         1♢ - 1♡   1♢ - 1♡
         1♣ - 1♡   1♣ - 1♡

    3. 1♠ - 2♣   4. 1♠ - 2♣
        1♡ - 3♡   1♡ - 2♣
        1♢ - 1♡   1♢ - 1♡
        1♣ - 1♡   1♣ - 1♡

    5. 1♠ - 1 NT
        1♡ - 2♡
        1♢ - 1♡
        1♣ - 1♡

67

Chapter 5

THINKING: MORE ON PLANNING THE PLAY OPENER'S REBID

THINKING: MORE ON PLANNING THE PLAY

Let's talk a little more about a good declarer's thought processes when he is PLANNING HIS PLAY. Once in a while, you may have nine top tricks to cash in 3 NT, or you may be able to claim an overtrick in your 4 ♠ contract by drawing trumps and conceding a couple of aces. Usually, though, there will be a few problems. For instance, it may be necessary for you to *develop* some tricks to make your contract. We have seen that there are many ways to do this: You can establish long cards or intermediates, take finesses, ruff losers in dummy, reverse the dummy, or even play for a double ruffing squeeze if you want to. But . . .

> YOU MUST HAVE A PLAN OF SOME KIND. DON'T
> START CASHING WINNERS AIMLESSLY; YOU MAY
> RUN OUT OF WINNERS BEFORE MAKING THE RE-
> QUIRED TRICKS. YOU MUST DO SOME PLANNING
> AND YOU MUST DO IT EARLY.

Here is a hand that appears in Edgar Kaplan's classic book, *Winning Contract Bridge Complete*. We know of no better illustration of the importance of declarer's planning.

```
              ♠ 9 5 3
              ♡ A 8 5 3
              ◇ J 10 7 5 3
              ♣ 6
  ♠ Q J 10        N        ♠ 4 2
  ♡ K J 9 7    W     E     ♡ Q 10 6 4
  ◇ K 4 2         S        ◇ 9 8 6
  ♣ 10 9 4                 ♣ K J 7 3
              ♠ A K 8 7 6
              ♡ 2
              ◇ A Q
              ♣ A Q 8 5 2
```

The contract is 4♠ and the ♠Q is led. Kaplan points out that declarer can try for his contract in many ways. He might:

(1) Set up diamonds. Win the opening lead, cash another high trump and play the ◊A and ◊Q. If someone wins the king, dummy's diamonds are good and entries to dummy remain.
(2) Ruff clubs. Win the first trick, play the ♣A and ruff a club. Cash the ♡A, ruff a heart and ruff another club. Come to hand with the ◊A, draw another trump and concede a trick to the ♣K if necessary.
(3) Take finesses in diamonds and clubs. Win the first trick, play to the ♡A and finesse the ♣Q. If that works, ruff a club and try the diamond finesse. If your finessing luck is in, you may do very well.
(4) Cross-ruff clubs and hearts. You may be able to ruff three hearts in your hand and two clubs in dummy. Five trumps plus your two high trumps and three side aces would add up to ten tricks.

Any of these plans might lead to success. Kaplan's point is that the actual declarer had muddled around. He won the first trick, took the ♡A and ruffed a heart, took the ♣A and ruffed a club, and tried the diamond finesse. West won and led a second trump, and declarer had to lose three more tricks for down one. Any reasonable plan would have succeeded, but declarer went down because he had *no* plan.

Counting your sure tricks as the main part of your planning will save you from going down on some easy hands.

1.   ♠ Q 6 5 3 2
                 ♡ K 7
                 ◊ 4
                 ♣ Q 8 6 4 2

                 ♠ 9 7
                 ♡ Q J 10 9 8
                 ◊ A 7 5 3
                 ♣ A J

You are declarer in a 2♡ contract and the ◊Q is led. You have four sure heart tricks, one diamond, and one club. Two extra tricks are available by ruffing two diamonds in dummy. So you ruff a diamond at trick two. Now you want to return to hand for another diamond ruff. You lead a club toward your hand and your right-hand

69

opponent plays low. **Would you finesse your ♣J at this point?** Certainly not. You can count eight tricks not including the ♣J. And if a club finesse lost to left-hand opponent, he would have a chance to lead trumps, preventing you from ruffing another diamond. Since you don't want to go down on an easy hand, win the ♣A and ruff another diamond.

2.
♠ A 9
♡ K J 2
◊ 5 4 3
♣ J 9 8 3 2

♠ K 7
♡ A Q 6 5
◊ A K 6 2
♣ Q 10 5

Suppose you are declarer with these cards in 3 NT. Plan the play against the ♠Q opening lead. **How many top tricks do you have?** You have eight top tricks and must develop one more. **How should you go about it?** Say you decide to go after clubs. The opponents win the first club. **What suit do they lead?** They return a spade, establishing *their* suit. **What happens if you lead a second club now?** The opponents win and cash their spades. One of them must have had at least five spades, so they now have three or more winners in spades plus their high clubs. Down at least one.

Do you see the trouble with trying to establish clubs? The *timing* is against you in that suit. After the opening lead, you have *one* spade stopper left and must knock out *two* high clubs to establish the suit. No good. You must look elsewhere in your planning.

What is the alternative? Suppose diamonds are 3-3. You can win the first trick and play three rounds of that suit, establishing a long card while you still have a spade stopper. This *isn't a sure thing*, but it is better than *no* chance.

Here are some other examples which require careful PLANNING by declarer. In each one declarer must begin, as usual, by *counting his sure winners*.

3.

    ♠ K 2
    ♡ K 3 2
    ◇ 9 7 6 4 2
    ♣ K 5 3

    ♠ A 5
    ♡ A Q 6 4
    ◇ A 8 5 3
    ♣ Q J 4

Contract: 3 NT
Opening lead: ♠Q

How many top tricks does declarer have? Six. He needs three
more. **What are the various possibilities?** Hearts may split 3-3, pro-
viding one extra trick; the ♣A can be knocked out, for two winners; the long diamonds can be established. **How will the diamond
suit have to split?** The suit will have to divide 2-2. **Why won't a
3-1 split be good enough?** By the time you concede *two* diamond
tricks, the opponents will have *their* suit established and cashed. **How
should you play this hand?**
    Suppose the hearts split 3-3. You would then have seven fast tricks,
right? In that case, you could play clubs and get *two* more winners.
But suppose hearts do *not* split and only three heart tricks are available.
Then it will do no good to play clubs, which would still leave you
a trick short. You would have to go after *diamonds,* hoping for a
2-2 split. You'd get *three* extra tricks and make nine altogether. So
after winning the first trick with a high spade, **what suit should you
play?** *Hearts.* You need to see how many heart tricks there are before
learning whether to play clubs or diamonds for your other tricks.

4.
          ♠ 4 3 2
          ♡ A Q
          ◇ Q 9 3 2
          ♣ A K 3 2

          ♠ A 8 6
          ♡ J 4 3
          ◇ A J 10 4
          ♣ Q 5 4

Contract: 3 NT (East overcalled in spades)
Opening lead: ♣ 10

Declarer begins by *ducking* the first round of spades, *holding up* his stopper to sever the opponents' communication. He wins the second spade and can count *six* top tricks. Extra tricks are available in diamonds and hearts (finesses to take), and clubs (long card if the suit is split 3-3). The diamond finesse must be attempted. If it works, you have *nine* tricks. If it loses, you will need either one of the other two chances to come home. **How should you play this hand?**

Suppose you take the diamond finesse right away. You will make the contract if it works, but let's be pessimistic and say it loses. (Apply Murphy's Law in these situations — whatever can go wrong, will.) West wins. Suppose he now returns . . . a heart. Do you see the problem? Declarer must decide *right now which* of his other chances he must try. He must decide whether clubs will split 3-3 or whether the heart finesse will work. West's heart return has effectively *deprived* declarer of the opportunity to try *both* chances at his leisure. Declarer can avoid this awkward dilemma by planning ahead. **Do you see how?** He should cash three rounds of clubs *before* taking the diamond finesse. When declarer sees how many club tricks are available, he will know if he must risk the heart finesse if the diamond finesse loses.

OPENER'S REBID

If the auction begins with a bid of one of a suit (a bid with a wide range of possible meanings), it may take several bids before the partnership can decide on an accurate contract. OPENER'S REBID can be an important part of the exchange because it is here that the player begins to use his *judgment* in selecting an action.

Suppose you have opened with one of a suit and your partner has responded. You must decide what to do next. There are two general cases to discuss.

CASE ONE:

An *important principle* in constructive bidding is that, *when one player has made a bid that limits his strength,* his partner becomes "captain" of the partnership and must see that the proper level is reached. The simplest example is when the opening bid is 1 NT. Responder must guide the auction because opener has limited and described his hand.

So, when responder's very first bid limits his strength, opener is "captain" and must try to place the contract, suggest a contract, try to improve the contract, or try for game.

You opened 1 ♠, and partner raised to 2 ♠:

1. ♠ A K J x x
    ♡ A x x
    ◇ Q x x
    ♣ x x

    Pass. Game is unlikely.

2. ♠ A K J x x
    ♡ A x x x
    ◇ A K
    ♣ x x

    4 ♠. Your hand is worth about 21 points, so you should have an excellent chance to make game even if partner has a minimum, 6-point raise.

3. ♠ K 9 x x x
    ♡ A J x
    ◇ A K J
    ♣ x x

    3 ♠, invitational to game. Partner must bid game or pass, depending on whether his raise is minimum or maximum.

You opened 1 ♠, and partner responded 1 NT:

4. ♠ A K x x x
    ♡ Q x x
    ◇ A x x
    ♣ J x

    Pass. Game is impossible, and you have no reason to think any better contract is available.

5. ♠ A K x x x
    ♡ x x
    ◇ x x
    ♣ A Q x x

    2 ♣. With a hand that looks unsuitable for notrump, try to improve the contract by offering partner another suit.

6. ♠ A K x x x   3 NT. Your hand is worth about 20
   ♡ K Q x   points, so game should have a chance
   ◊ A x   even if partner has only 6. Notrump looks
   ♣ K 10 x   best from your point of view.

7. ♠ A K x x x x   2 ♠. Note that you should have a *six*-card
   ♡ K x x   suit (or longer) to make this bid. Remem-
   ◊ x   ber, partner may have only one spade or
   ♣ K J x   even none at all.

8. ♠ A K J x x x   3 ♠. This shows a good six-card (or
   ♡ A x x   longer) suit and 16-18 high-card points.
   ◊ K J x   Partner is invited to bid on but may pass
   ♣ x   with a minimum response.

You opened 1 ♣ , and partner responded 2 NT:

9. ♠ K 10 x x x   3 NT. You can place the contract.
   ♡ A x x
   ◊ K x
   ♣ A x x

10. ♠ A K x x x   3 ♣. You shouldn't be so anxious to com-
    ♡ x x   mit the hand to the notrump game. Re-
    ◊ x x   member that the auction is forcing to game
    ♣ A Q x x   after partner's 2 NT, so you can afford
                 to show your doubts about notrump. Part-
ner can insist on notrump, support spades, raise clubs, or bid three
of a red suit with a concentration of high cards in that suit.

You opened 1 ♣ , and partner responded 3 NT:

11. ♠ K Q 10 x x   Bid 6 NT. This is what your hand is
    ♡ A x x   clearly worth, so don't shirk your respon-
    ◊ A Q x   sibility.
    ♣ Q x

In each of these examples, *opener knew how many points responder
had from his first response.* He could place the contract immediately; invite a contract; or mark time, hoping to place the contract accurately later. But opener was "captain."

CASE TWO:

Suppose you opened with one of a suit and your partner responded with a suit of his own. For instance:

Opener	*Responder*
1 ◇	1 ♠

What kind of hand does responder have? At least 6 points and at least a four-card suit are the *minimum* requirements, aren't they? But responder could have many more than 6 points and he could have a much stronger suit. We can't know the *upper* limit of his hand at this point. **Is there any way opener could hope to place the contract accurately at this point?** No way at all. If the response had been *2 ◇*, opener could take over, but as it is, he cannot know the best contract. In *this* case:

Opener will continue to describe his hand, hoping that responder can become "captain." Many different types of hands can be opened 1 ◇, so opener has many ways to tell more about the features of his hand.

You opened 1 ◇, and partner responded 1 ♠:

1. ♠ x
   ♡ A x x
   ◇ K Q x x x x
   ♣ A x x

   2 ◇. Minimum hand (13-15) with *long* diamonds. You typically have six or more cards to rebid your suit here. You *may* rebid a suit of only five cards, but then there may be a more attractive option — another suit you can bid or a notrump bid.

2. ♠ x
   ♡ A x x
   ◇ A K J x x x
   ♣ A x x

   3 ◇. Extra strength (16-18) and six or more good diamonds. Partner is invited to bid on but may pass with a minimum.

3. ♠ x x
   ♡ Q x
   ◇ A K x x x
   ♣ A J x x

   2 ♣. This gives you the option of playing in the suit your partner prefers. Do not rebid 2 ◇ (to show five). You might miss a superior club fit. (Partner should credit you with longer diamonds than clubs on this auction anyway, since you would open *1 ♣* with four cards in each suit.)

4. ♠ x x   3♣. A jump shift by opener is forcing to
    ♡ A x   game. If the ◊ K were a low diamond,
    ◊ A K J x x   you would rebid just 2♣ despite your
    ♣ A K x x   extra strength.

5. ♠ K x x x   2♠. You prefer *four-card support* to raise
    ♡ x x   partner here, since he may have suggested
    ◊ A Q x x   spades with a poor four-card suit. With a
    ♣ A x x   minimum opening, you raise to *two* only.

6. ♠ K Q x x   3♠. Extra strength (16-18) and four-card
    ♡ x x   support for partner's suit. Notice that part-
    ◊ A K x x x   ner's response may *improve* the value of
    ♣ A x   your hand.

7. ♠ K Q x x   4♠. Partner should make it even if he has
    ♡ x x   only 6 points and four poorish spades. (If
    ◊ A K Q x   he has more, he may bid some more.)
    ♣ A Q x

8. ♠ x x   1 NT. When you rebid notrump at the
    ♡ Q J x   cheapest level, you show a balanced,
    ◊ A Q x x x   minimum opening. Note that you do not
    ♣ A J x   rebid the diamond suit. A notrump rebid
                        describes your hand more accurately.

9. ♠ x x   2 NT. A jump in notrump shows 19-20
    ♡ A J x   points and balanced pattern. Partner will
    ◊ A K J x x   pass only if he has a very minimum re-
    ♣ A Q x   sponse.

Let's look at some of the problems opener may encounter in making his rebid.

You opened 1 ◊ , and partner responded 1♠:

1. ♠ A J x   With this minimum hand, your second bid
    ♡ x   should be 2♠ despite the lack of four-card
    ◊ A x x x x   support. This is not a bad hand for play
    ♣ K J x x   at spades, with your ruffing power in
                        hearts.

2. ♠ K x
   ♡ x
   ◇ A K J x x x
   ♣ A J x x

Should you rebid 3◇ or 2♣? 2♣ is more "flexible" (it saves more space). You can rebid diamonds at your next turn, implying a nice hand with six diamonds and four clubs.

3. ♠ x x
   ♡ x
   ◇ A K J x x x
   ♣ A J x x

With this minimum, limit your strength right away with a 2◇ rebid.

4. ♠ K Q x x
   ♡ x
   ◇ A K J x x
   ♣ A Q x

This hand is worth 4♠, but you should not bid it directly. Jump to 3♣ (forcing as it is a jump shift), and bid 4♠ next. Partner will know you are *very short* in the suit you have *not* bid. If he happens to be interested in a *slam,* this knowledge may help him decide whether to bid it. (If he has the ♡A opposite your known shortness, that would be just right.)

5. ♠ x x
   ♡ A J x x
   ◇ K Q x x
   ♣ A x x

Here you must decide whether to bid 2♡, showing your other suit, or 1 NT, showing a balanced minimum. In general, you want to get all your suits into the auction so you can find a fit. There is a special consideration here, however, because of the *order in which you would have to show your suits.* Here we meet the important concept of the REVERSE.

THE REVERSE:

Let's move over to responder's side of the table for a minute. Say that partner opens 1◇, and you scrape up a 1♡ response on:

♠ x x x
♡ A Q x x
◇ x x x x
♣ x x

Partner rebids 2♣. Of course, you are not interested in game, but you cannot pass 2♣ when *diamonds* is clearly a better trump suit. Take a *preference* to 2◇, getting your side back to its best trump suit.

Now suppose this is your hand:

♠ x x x
♡ A Q x x
◊ x x
♣ x x x x

Here you can take a preference by passing, since clubs is fine and you don't want to go further. (Game is impossible.) Note that when partner shows his suits beginning with the higher-ranking, you can play in either one at the two level, as you prefer.

Now let's look at a different auction. Partner opens 1 ♣, you scrape up 1 ♡ on your:

♠ x x x
♡ A Q x x
◊ x x
♣ x x x x

Partner now rebids 2 ◊. No choice, you must get your side back to its clearly better trump suit. But to bid clubs, you must go to the level of three. *The order in which partner showed his suits leaves you no option but to play at a higher contract.*

So who, in this situation, must bear the responsibility for the partnership's arrival at a nine-trick contract? *Opener* must be prepared to play at the three level on this auction.

NOTE THIS WELL: In an auction like:

Opener	Responder
1 ◊	1 ♠
2 ♡	

or

1 ♡	2 ♣
2 ♠	

responder, if he prefers the first of the two suits that opener offered, must do so at the *three* level. Opener's bidding says, in effect, that he feels safe at the three level if responder prefers his first suit. These auctions are examples of a REVERSE by opener. They suggest *extra strength* in opener's hand.

Let's return to our original problem hand:

5. ♠ x x   Rebid 1 NT, not 2 ♡. A 2 ♡ rebid might
   ♡ A J x x   get you a *3 ◇* preference, and a three-level
   ◇ K Q x x   contract may not be safe.
   ♣ A x x

A rebid in notrump really looks more realistic on this hand. This is a balanced hand, after all, not a heart-diamond hand. (Note of interest: you will not automatically lose a heart fit if you rebid 1 NT. If partner has only four spades, he cannot have four hearts — he would respond 1 ♡ with four of each major, remember — but if he has five spades and four hearts, he will bid 2 ♡ over your 1 NT with his unbalanced hand.)

6. ♠ x x   A 2 ♡ rebid *here* is fine. You will be safe
   ♡ A Q x x   (and may bid further) if partner prefers
   ◇ A K x x x   diamonds.
   ♣ A x

7. ♠ x x   Rebid 2 NT. A REVERSE always implies
   ♡ A Q x x   *a two-suited hand,* with *greater length in*
   ◇ A K J x   *your first suit.*
   ♣ A J x

8. ♠ x x   2 ♣. *Avoiding a reverse* with your mini-
   ♡ A x   mum was what you had in mind when you
   ◇ A K J x   opened *1 ◇* instead of your longer club
   ♣ Q x x x x   suit.

A miscellaneous situation:

9. ♠ A K 6 5 4   This hand is often mishandled. Some
   ♡ A Q J 6 5   players want to open 1 ♡ so they can re-
   ◇ A 6   verse into 2 ♠. Remember, a reverse im-
   ♣ 4   plies greater length in your *first* suit.
                    Describe this hand by opening 1 ♠, then
                    jumping in hearts.

To sum up, REVERSES, so called because opener *reverses* the usual order of showing his two suits (higher-ranking first is the preferred order, remember), promise extra strength, about 17 high-card points or more.

OPENER'S REBID — after an opening suit bid and a response:

CASE ONE — *If responder has made a bid that limits his strength:*

PASS —	If no game contract is possible and you are satisfied with the contract.
TRY TO IMPROVE THE CONTRACT —	If partner responds 1 NT, you may suggest another suit if your hand looks unsuitable for notrump.
TRY FOR GAME —	If responder limited his hand and there may be a game depending on whether he is minimum or maximum for his bidding.
FORCE TO GAME —	By jumping in a new suit.
BID GAME —	If you know the values for game are present and which game contract is best.

CASE TWO — *If responder bids a new suit* — opener must describe his hand further:

REBID THE MINIMUM NUMBER OF NOTRUMP — with 13-15 high-card points and balanced pattern. This bid denies another suit you could show at the one level as well as four-card support for partner's suit.

JUMP ONE LEVEL IN NOTRUMP — with 19-20 and balanced pattern. With a balanced 21 points, you would jump all the way to 3 NT.

RAISE PARTNER'S SUIT ONE LEVEL — with 13-15 points and four-card support (rarely, three-card support).

RAISE PARTNER'S SUIT TWO LEVELS — with 16-18 points and four-card support.

RAISE PARTNER'S SUIT TO GAME — with 19-20 points and four-card support.

If you hold a second suit of four or more cards —

BID YOUR SECOND SUIT — as cheaply as possible with 13-18 points***

JUMP IN YOUR SECOND SUIT — with 19 points or more. This bid, a jump shift, is forcing (to game).

If you hold just one long suit —

REBID YOUR LONG SUIT — as cheaply as possible with 13-15 points.

JUMP IN YOUR LONG SUIT — with 16-18 points. This bid suggests a good six or seven-card suit.

In theory, you may REBID any suit of five or more cards. Avoid doing so, however, if there is an alternative. Rebid in notrump if your hand is balanced or show another suit

---

***See, however, the materials on REVERSES.

TEST YOUR COMPREHENSION OF THE MATERIAL IN THIS CHAPTER:

QUIZ ON PLANNING THE PLAY AS DECLARER:

1.
♠ 6 5 4 3
♡ A 9
◇ Q 5 4
♣ 7 6 5 4

♠ A K Q
♡ J 4
◇ A K 3 2
♣ A Q 8 2

Contract: 3 NT
Opening lead: ♡ 7
Plan the play.

2.
♠ Q J 2
♡ 4 3 2
◇ A 7 6 5 4
♣ A Q

♠ A K 10 9 7 3
♡ A 8 7
◇ 8 3
♣ 5 4

Contract: 4 ♠
Opening lead: ♣ 2
Plan the play.

3.
♠ 4 3
♡ K J 5
◇ J 6 5
♣ A Q 7 5 4

♠ A 10 2
♡ A Q 10 7 3
◇ 8 3 2
♣ K 8

Contract: 4 ♡
Opening lead: ◇ A
The opponents cash three diamond tricks and shift to a spade.
Plan the play.

82

SOLUTIONS:

1. Declarer has eight top tricks and many chances for a ninth. He should plan the play so he can try *every* possible chance. He ducks the opening lead, in case West has led from a heart suit headed by the king-queen. Assuming East wins and returns a heart, declarer wins and test spades. If the suit split 3-3, the ◊ Q is an entry to the long card.

    If spades fail to break, declarer tries diamonds next. He cashes three rounds *ending in dummy.* If the suit splits 3-3, declarer plays a club to his ace, and takes his good diamond.

    If diamonds fail to split, declarer must fall back on the club finesse as his last chance, and the lead is in dummy so he can lead a club to his queen. (The club play should be the last resort, since the defenders will cash hearts if they get in. It costs declarer nothing, however, to test the spades and diamonds.)

2. Declarer should *win the ♣A* and rely on diamonds. A losing club finesse at trick one will lead to a certain set when the defenders switch to hearts.

    Declarer's chances of setting up a diamond trick are excellent. He ducks a diamond at trick two to keep all his entries to dummy available. The defense will win, cash the ♣K, and lead a heart. Declarer wins, plays ◊ A, ruffs a diamond with a high trump, leads a trump to dummy and ruffs another diamond high. The fifth diamond in dummy will be a winner now, even if an opponent began with four diamonds.

    Declarer now draws two more rounds of trumps, *ending in dummy,* and cashes his good diamond. (If diamonds split 3-3, only one diamond needs to be ruffed and declarer makes an overtrick.)

3. If trumps split 3-2, declarer can afford to ruff a club (high) in his hand to cater to a 4-2 club break. If trumps are 4-1, declarer must hope clubs split 3-3, since he cannot ruff a club and draw trumps ending in dummy. Since all depends on the trump suit, declarer should test it first by playing the ace and jack. If trumps are 4-1, declarer draws all the trumps and plays three high clubs. If defenders follow to two trumps, the play continues: ♣K, ♣A, club ruff high, ♡K, ♣Q, club.

QUIZ ON OPENER'S REBID:

I. You opened 1♠, partner responded 2♢.

    1. ♠ A K Q x x   2. ♠ A Q x x x
        ♡ A x x   ♡ K x x
        ♢ x x   ♢ J x
        ♣ x x x   ♣ K J x

    3. ♠ A Q J x x   4. ♠ A J 10 x x
        ♡ K J x x   ♡ A K
        ♢ x   ♢ x
        ♣ Q x x   ♣ Q x x x x

    5. ♠ A Q J x x x
        ♡ A x x
        ♢ A x
        ♣ Q x

II. You opened 1♡, partner responded 2♡.

    1. ♠ A Q   2. ♠ A x
        ♡ A J x x x   ♡ A J x x x
        ♢ K Q x   ♢ A Q x x
        ♣ K J x   ♣ K x

    3. ♠ A x
        ♡ A K J x x
        ♢ A x x
        ♣ x x x

III. You opened 1♣, partner responded 1♡.

    1. ♠ Q x x   2. ♠ A Q J x
        ♡ x x   ♡ x x
        ♢ A K x x   ♢ A x
        ♣ A J x x   ♣ A J x x x

    3. ♠ A x   4. ♠ A x
        ♡ x x   ♡ x x
        ♢ A K J x   ♢ Q x x x
        ♣ A Q x x x   ♣ A K J x x

5. ♠ x x
    ♡ K x x x
    ◇ A x
    ♣ A Q x x x

6. ♠ x
    ♡ K x x
    ◇ A x x
    ♣ A K Q x x x

7. ♠ x x
    ♡ A K x x
    ◇ Q x
    ♣ A K x x x

8. ♠ x x
    ♡ A Q x x
    ◇ A x x
    ♣ A K Q x

9. ♠ A J x
    ♡ K x x
    ◇ K x x
    ♣ A K J x

10. ♠ A K J x
    ♡ x x
    ◇ A x
    ♣ A K x x x

IV. You opened 1 ♠, partner responded 1 NT.

1. ♠ A K J x x x
    ♡ Q x x x
    ◇ K x
    ♣ x

2. ♠ A K Q x x x
    ♡ Q x
    ◇ K x x
    ♣ Q x

3. ♠ A Q x x x
    ♡ A x x
    ◇ x
    ♣ K J x x

4. ♠ A K J x x
    ♡ A x x
    ◇ x
    ♣ A Q J x

5. ♠ K J x x x
    ♡ A x x
    ◇ A x
    ♣ Q x x

85

SOLUTIONS:

I. 1. 2♠
    2. 2 NT (showing a balanced minimum)
    3. 2♡
    4. 2♠ (3♣ would be a reverse, promising more in high cards)
    5. 3♠

II. 1. 3 NT (partner can always return to hearts if his hand is unbalanced)
    2. 4♡
    3. 3♡

III. 1. 1 NT (*not* 2◊, which would be a reverse)
     2. 1♠
     3. 2◊ (you have adequate strength for a reverse)
     4. 2♣ (you would prefer another club, but there is no choice)
     5. 2♡
     6. 3♣
     7. 3♡
     8. 4♡
     9. 2 NT
    10. 2♠

IV. 1. 2♠
    2. 2 NT (3♠ is possible, but this hand is notrump-oriented)
    3. 2♣
    4. 3♣
    5. Pass

Chapter 6

THINKING:
DEFENSE: WHICH SUITS TO LEAD; SIGNALS
RESPONDER'S REBID AND PLACING
THE CONTRACT

THINKING: DEFENSE — WHICH SUITS TO LEAD; SIGNALS

In the next few chapters, we will look at how a good *defender's* thought processes work. In an elementary bridge book, you learn rules that govern defensive play. Rules are necessary at that stage because you don't have enough experience to *judge* every situation that comes along. But now you can start learning how to rely on your *judgment*. Specifically, we will look at the problem of *what suit you should lead.*

1.

♠ K 5 3
♡ A J
◇ K Q J 9 4
♣ 10 4 3

♠ A J 9 7 4
♡ K 7 6 4
◇ 10 3
♣ A 5

South	West	North	East
1 ♣	Pass	1 ◇	1 ♠
2 ♣	2 ♠	3 NT	Pass
4 ♣	Pass	5 ♣	(All Pass)

Partner leads the ♠ 2, dummy's king is played, and you win the ace. **What should you do now?**

Relying on a defensive rule, you might choose to *return* a spade UP TO WEAKNESS here. However . . . **How many spades do you think declarer has, based on his refusal to play 3 NT?** No more than one. If partner has the ◇ A, are there any worries? No, the defense will surely get three tricks. Suppose *declarer* has the ◇ A (declarer opened the bidding, remember). **In what suit must the defense take a trick to set 5 ♣?** Right, *hearts.* **Can you expect your**

♡ **K to be worth a trick eventually?** No, declarer will run dummy's diamonds and *throw away* his little hearts. If you are to take a heart trick, it must be *swiftly*. **What card must partner have in hearts?** The queen. You must lead a heart immediately and hope to set up a trick before declarer can draw trumps and take his diamond tricks.

♠ Q 10 6 2
♡ Q 9 8 3
◊ 8 7 6 5
♣ 8

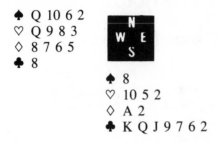

♠ 8
♡ 10 5 2
◊ A 2
♣ K Q J 9 7 6 2

This is a good time to disregard rules and lead toward dummy's *strength*. With all those diamond tricks in sight, you have nothing to lose by *taking a chance* with a heart lead. You must *get busy*. Now let's look at a different situation.

2.   ♠ J 10 4
            ♡ K 10 3
            ◊ 6 5 4 3
            ♣ A 7 5

♠ Q 6
♡ J 8 7 4
◊ K 8 7
♣ Q 10 8 2

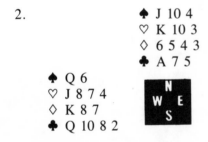

South, the declarer, opened 1 ♣; North responded 2 ♣; South rebid 3 ♣, and everyone passed. You choose to lead the ♣2. Dummy plays low, and partner wins the ♣K and returns the jack. Declarer wins the ace and finesses the ♣J, losing to your queen. All follow to your ♣Q. **What should you lead now?**

A club lead would be dangerous, since it would allow declarer to *ruff* in dummy and *discard* a loser from his hand. Should you lead a heart *through strength?* Consider this: *If declarer has losing hearts in his hand, is there any way he can get rid of them?* Not when the dummy is *flat* and *weak*. (Contrast with the dummy on the *first* hand.) Therefore the defense has no reason to hurry to collect their heart (or diamond) tricks. They can afford to *wait*. The best exit here, a trump, is *safe*. It will give declarer nothing that is not his for the taking anyway.

♠ 8 5 2
♡ Q 6 5
◊ J 10 9 2
♣ K J 6

♠ A K 9 7 3
♡ A 9 2
◊ A Q
♣ 9 4 3

Note that you will cost your side a trick if you lead either red suit.

Even though trumps is usually declarer's best suit, the defense may find it a good suit to lead, for *safety*. Here is another example.

3.

♠ 9 7 5 3 2
♡ K 6 5 3
◊ A 9 8
♣ 3

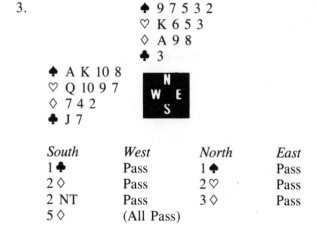

♠ A K 10 8
♡ Q 10 9 7
◊ 7 4 2
♣ J 7

South	West	North	East
1 ♣	Pass	1 ♠	Pass
2 ◊	Pass	2 ♡	Pass
2 NT	Pass	3 ◊	Pass
5 ◊	(All Pass)		

You lead the ♠A, partner follows low, and declarer drops the jack. **What should you lead now?**

This time the dummy doesn't have much help for declarer. Not many high cards and no good suit to establish. There are, however, some *ruffing* tricks available. Declarer will try to make all his trumps separately by ruffing clubs in dummy (and spades in his hand). So you lead a trump, drawing *two* of his trumps for one of yours.

♠ Q 6 4
♡ J 8
◇ 10 6 3
♣ Q 10 8 5 2

♠ J
♡ A 4 2
◇ K Q J 5
♣ A K 9 6 4

Note that if you do not draw a round of trumps, declarer will make seven trump tricks and his contract.

Let's review the ideas we have seen so far:

1. Defensive rules must occasionally be broken.
2. If the dummy is *very strong* and will provide declarer with several *discards* for his losers, *try to set up a fast trick,* even if it means taking a chance.
3. If the dummy is *weak,* without much help for declarer, lead a *safe* suit, one that *cannot give away* a trick.
4. If the dummy has *ruffing* power, consider leading a *trump.*

Luckily, there are times when you won't have to decide what to lead by working from general principles. *Your partner may have a chance to tell you what to do.* The *card that he plays* can, in some circumstances, be used as a *signal.*

Let's look at a defensive problem that would be difficult to solve without the use of *defensive signals.*

4.   ♠ K 8 5 3
            ♡ A
            ◇ K 7 5
            ♣ J 9 6 4 2

♠ 7 2
♡ Q 10 7 4 2
◇ J 10 4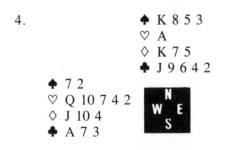
♣ A 7 3

The opponents arrive at 3 NT, against which you lead the ♡4. Dummy wins, and declarer leads a club to his queen and your ace. **What should you lead now?**

There is really no way to tell! Partner could have either:

(a)	♠ J 10 9 4		(b)	♠ J 10 9 4
	♡ K 8 3			♡ 8 5 3
	◊ Q 9 6 3 2	or		◊ A Q 9 6 3
	♣ 8			♣ 8

Defensive signals will help. When you lead a heart and dummy wins, partner must tell you whether he wants you to lead that suit again or try another suit. He does this by playing the *HIGHEST* heart spot he can afford to show *ENCOURAGEMENT,* but his *LOWEST* spot to suggest a *SWITCH.* With hand (a) above, he would follow with his ♡ 8 at trick one, and you would know to continue. With hand (b), he would play his *three,* and you would lead diamonds, the most attractive suit besides hearts.

This signal, called ATTITUDE, is one of several signals the defenders may find useful. Since what suits to lead or continue leading is the most common problem the defenders face, the ATTITUDE signal is the most important one to know about.

ATTITUDE is also used routinely in defending against *suit* contracts. Suppose your partner leads the ♡ A against a 4 ♠ contract. Your heart holding is K-Q-9-7-2. You might play your *nine,* requesting partner to lead more hearts. (*Don't* play the *seven,* which might not be as clear to partner.) If you had ♡ 972, you would play your *two,* showing no interest.

The ATTITUDE signal is also used in *discarding.* If you were defending 4 ♠ and you wished to *discard* from ♡ KQ972, you might throw your *nine,* suggesting strength in hearts. Partner would know this was a good suit for him to lead. Beware, however, of signalling your strength to partner too readily. If you signal the location of an ace, for example, the information may be put to use by *declarer,* who can see your signals also. Signal only if you feel partner needs the information.

Defending against a suit contract, you may show interest in a suit even if you have no *high* cards there. Look at this hand:

5.

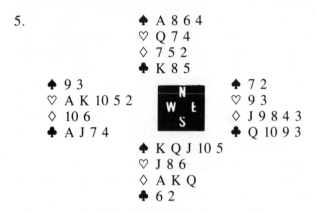

        ♠ A 8 6 4
        ♡ Q 7 4
        ◊ 7 5 2
        ♣ K 8 5

♠ 9 3   ♠ 7 2
♡ A K 10 5 2   ♡ 9 3
◊ 10 6   ◊ J 9 8 4 3
♣ A J 7 4   ♣ Q 10 9 3

        ♠ K Q J 10 5
        ♡ J 8 6
        ◊ A K Q
        ♣ 6 2

South is declarer at 4 ♠, after West overcalled in hearts. The opening lead is the ♡A, and East must play the *nine,* asking for a continuation. He hopes to ruff the third round. When this happens the contract goes down one. Without a signal to guide him, West might shift to a minor suit at the second trick.

One thing to keep in mind in your signalling: The size of the spots is relative, not absolute. A *four* may show encouragement if played from A-K-4-2, while an *eight* may be your lowest if you have 10-9-8. You must look at the spots in your own hand, in dummy, and the ones played by declarer and try to *interpret* the message partner is sending.

To sum up . . . *ATTITUDE,* one of several types of signals the defenders use, helps them decide what suits they should lead or continue to lead. You often show your ATTITUDE about your partner's suit as he leads it (although you may have to play "third-hand high" instead). You may also show your AT-TITUDE about a suit as you discard from that suit. A HIGH CARD ENCOURAGES A CONTINUATION OF THE SUIT LED OR SHOWS STRENGTH IN THAT SUIT, A LOW CARD SHOWS NO INTEREST OR WEAKNESS.

RESPONDER'S REBID AND PLACING THE CONTRACT

OPENER'S REBID will often tell how much high-card strength he has and suggest more about his distribution; so responder, by his second turn, may have a good idea of the best contract. *If opener limits his hand with his rebid, responder is captain.* He bears the responsibility of fixing the contract at the proper level.

A. *Opener*   *Responder*
   1 ♢   1 ♠   ♠ K J x x
   1 NT   ♡ A x x
                     ♢ Q x x
                     ♣ K x x

Bid 3 NT. Opener's sequence shows a balanced hand with 13-15 high-card points, so you know just where you want to play.

B. *Opener*   *Responder*
   1 ♠   2 ♣   ♠ A J x
   2 ♠   ♡ x x
                     ♢ A x x
                     ♣ Q x x x x

Bid 3 ♠. Opener shows a minimum hand with long spades. Game is possible, but only if opener has closer to a *15-point maximum.* Your 3 ♠ bid invites opener to go on to game if he likes his hand.

C. *Opener*   *Responder*
   1 ♡   1 ♠   ♠ K Q x x
   2 ♡   ♡ x
                     ♢ J x x x
                     ♣ Q x x x

Pass (before things get worse). Partner has a minimum with long hearts, so game is impossible and 2 ♡ is as good a spot as any.

In these three examples, opener made a minimum rebid, and responder bid game, invited game or passed, depending on how much strength *he* had. These hands illustrate the PRINCIPLE we apply for RESPONDER'S REBID.

> AT RESPONDER'S SECOND TURN, HE OFTEN BIDS THE
> LIMIT OF HIS VALUES (AS HIGH AS HE FEELS IT IS
> SAFE TO GO), TRYING TO PLACE THE CONTRACT OR
> SUGGEST A CONTRACT.

To illustrate this principle further, let's look at another example auction:

Opener	Responder
1 ◇	1 ♡
1 ♠	

Opener's bidding promises length in spades and diamonds (possibly four cards in each suit, perhaps longer diamonds). He *could* have a hand almost worth a jump to *2 ♠* but may have as few as 12 high-card points. Based on that knowledge, responder will BID WHAT HE THINKS HE CAN MAKE, THE *LIMIT* OF HIS HAND, IN PLACING THE CONTRACT OR SUGGESTING A CONTRACT Here is a list of options:

WITH WEAKNESS (6-9 points):	PASS, if you are satisfied to play right where you are. TAKE A PREFERENCE to the first suit opener showed. REBID YOUR OWN SUIT CHEAPLY with a six-card suit or longer. BID 1 NT with a balanced hand and no liking for any suit.
WITH INVITATIONAL VALUES (10-12 points):	RAISE partner's second suit, RAISE his first suit if he has rebid it, or RERAISE in your own suit (if partner raised you.) TAKE A JUMP PREFERENCE to opener's first suit. JUMP REBID IN YOUR OWN SUIT with a good six-card suit or longer. BID 2 NT.
WITH GAME-GOING VALUES (13 points or (slightly more):	JUMP TO GAME in one of partner's suits, in your own suit, or in notrump. BID A NEW SUIT (an exception to our principle), forcing opener to describe his hand *more* fully.

This table of options assumes that opener has made a MINIMUM rebid. If his rebid shows EXTRA STRENGTH, responder may bid game with correspondingly *less* strength. Using the example auction above, choose responder's rebid:

1. ♠ J x x x   Pass. Game is very unlikely, and spades is
   ♡ A x x x   the right strain.
   ◇ x x x
   ♣ J x

2. ♠ x x   Bid 2 ◇. In spite of your weakness, you
   ♡ A x x x   must bid again and get your side back to
   ◇ x x x x   its best trump suit.
   ♣ K x x

3. ♠ x x   Bid 2 ♡. You prefer a six-card suit for this
   ♡ K Q x x x x action, since partner may have to give up
   ◇ Q x   and pass with a minimum hand and a
   ♣ x x x   singleton heart.

4. ♠ x x   Bid 1 NT. This is only an attempt to im-
   ♡ K J x x   prove the contract. It shows weakness.
   ◇ x x x
   ♣ K J x x

Let's give responder a little better hand.

5. ♠ K Q x x   Bid 3 ♠. This is a good illustration of the
   ♡ A Q x x   PRINCIPLE we apply to responder's
   ◇ x x   rebid. Responder has bid the limit of his
   ♣ x x x   hand. His message is plain: "Partner, I
               am willing to play 3 ♠ even if your open-
ing bid is very minimum. If you have a little extra strength, please
go on to game." (Do not confuse this situation with a *direct* double
raise, which is *forcing*. Remember, at responder's *second* turn, he
bids the *limit* of his hand.)

6. ♠ x x   Bid 3 ◇. Game is possible if partner can
   ♡ A Q x x   bid again over your invitation. Do not bid
   ◇ K Q x x   2 ◇. That would show weakness and *no*
   ♣ x x x   interest in game.

7. ♠ x x   Bid 2 NT.
    ♥ K Q x x
    ♦ x x x
    ♣ A Q 10 x

8. ♠ x x   Bid 3 ♥. If partner has extra strength or a
    ♥ A Q J x x x fit for hearts, you wish to play game.
    ♦ A x
    ♣ x x x

After all of these INVITATIONAL actions by responder, opener must look at his hand again and decide whether to bid further.

Now suppose that responder has an opening bid (or slightly more) himself. Now he wants to reach game no matter what sort of opening bid his partner has.

9. ♠ K Q x x   Bid 4 ♠.
    ♥ A x x x
    ♦ A x
    ♣ x x x

10. ♠ J x   Bid 3 NT.
    ♥ A K x x
    ♦ Q x x
    ♣ K 10 x x

11. ♠ A x   Bid 4 ♥.
    ♥ A Q J 10 x x
    ♦ Q x
    ♣ x x x

We saw that responder may be obliged to take a PREFERENCE if he thinks that the *first* suit opener offered will be the better trump suit. The idea of showing a tolerance for partner's suits is important:

Opener	Responder	
1 ♠	2 ♣	♠ J x x
2 ♥		♥ x x
		♦ A x x
		♣ K Q x x x

Bid 2 ♠. Partner would like to know you have three-card support.

Opener	Responder	
1 ◇	1 ♠	♠ A K x x
2 ♣		♡ x x x
		◇ x x x
		♣ x x x

Bid 2 ◇. Partner probably has longer diamonds, so it is your duty to take a preference.

Opener	Responder	
1 ♡	1 ♠	♠ A x x x x
2 ♣		♡ J x
		◇ x x x x
		♣ Q x

Bid 2 ♡. 2 ♠ or 2 ◇ (which fails to limit your hand) could lead to disaster. Partner should realize that you have only a doubleton heart, since with weakness (6-9) and three hearts, you would have raised at your first turn.

♠ A J x x x
♡ Q x
◇ x x x
♣ J x x

Bid 2 ♡. Playing in a *5-2* fit is often preferable to a *4-3*. Your preference will give opener another chance to bid if he has extra strength.

Quite often, it will be *responder* who has two suits to show and would like to hear opener take a preference for one of them:

Opener	Responder	
1 ◇	1 ♡	♠ A x x x
2 ♣		♡ A Q x x x
		◇ K x
		♣ x x

You could jump to 3 NT, but it might be the wrong contract, especially if opener has three hearts and a singleton spade. 2 ♠, a new suit, is forcing and will get you some more information. Opener should bid 3 ♡ now with three-card support. If he does this, you can bid game in hearts. If opener bids 2 NT or repeats one of his minor suits, take your chances in 3 NT.

```
♠ A J x x
♡ A K x x
◇ x x
♣ J x x
```

Bid 3 NT. There is no point in bidding 2 ♠ here, since you are not
interested in knowing if partner can take a heart preference. You
can just place the contract.

Opener	Responder	
1 ♠	2 ♡	♠ x x
2 ♠		♡ A K x x x
		◇ A Q x
		♣ x x x

Bid 3 ◇ (!) Perhaps partner can bid 3 NT or support your hearts. If
he bids his spades a third time, you will raise.

Opener	Responder	
1 ♡	1 ♠	♠ A J x x x
2 ♣		♡ x
		◇ x x x
		♣ K x x x

This is a big headache in our system. *Opener's change of suit* covers
a *wide range* of hands, so responder must *guess* whether to raise.
If opener has 17 points, responder may miss a game by passing. But
if he raises, opener may go on with 15 points (often, to 3 NT) and
get too high. There is no good solution. Be influenced by how good
your *support* for partner is, and whether your side strength is in
primary values (aces and kings).

*RESPONDER WILL
FREQUENTLY BE THE
"CAPTAIN" OF THE
PARTNERSHIP.*

98

So far, we have had opener make a *minimum* rebid at his second turn. If opener's rebid shows *extra* strength, responder needs *less* strength to bid aggressively.

Opener	Responder	
1 ♡	1 ♠	♠ A Q x x x
3 ♡		♡ K x
		◇ x x x x
		♣ x x

Bid 4 ♡. Opener shows 16-18 points and six or more good hearts. You have enough strength for game and your heart support is adequate when partner is known to have an excellent six-card suit.

Opener	Responder	
1 ◇	1 ♠	♠ K Q x x x
3 ♠		♡ x x
		◇ K x x
		♣ x x x

Bid 4 ♠. Opener shows 16-18 points in support of your suit. Since your hand is worth about 9 points, go on to game.

There is one more situation we need to look at. Sometimes, *responder will be the one to limit his hand* (at his first turn). From then on, his job will be to accept or reject game tries; show a suit he had to suppress earlier or prefer one of opener's suits; or make some further descriptive bid.

Opener	Responder	
1 ♡	2 ♡	♠ x x
3 ♡		♡ K J x x
		◇ A x x x
		♣ x x x

Bid 4 ♡. Opener's reraise was a try for game, asking whether you have a minimum or maximum raise. Yours could not be much better.

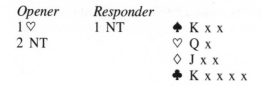

Opener	Responder
1 ♡	1 NT
2 NT	

♠ K x x
♡ Q x
◊ J x x
♣ K x x x x

Bid 3 NT, accepting partner's invitation with your maximum notrump response.

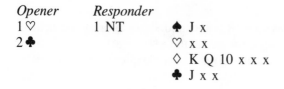

Opener	Responder
1 ♡	1 NT
2 ♣	

♠ J x
♡ x x
◊ K Q 10 x x x
♣ J x x

Bid 2 ◊. This suggests at least a *six*-card suit in your weak hand.

TEST YOUR COMPREHENSION OF THE MATERIAL IN THIS CHAPTER:

QUIZ ON YOUR DEFENSIVE STRATEGY:

1.

                ♠ 7 6 4
                ♡ J 10
                ◊ A K 5 4
                ♣ 8 6 4 3
♠ Q 8 3
♡ 7 4 3
◊ Q J 10 8
♣ J 7 5

South opened 1 ♡, North responded 1 NT, South jumped to 4 ♡, all passed. You lead the ◊ Q. Declarer wins the ace and cashes the king, discarding a low club. He then leads a spade to his ten and your queen. What do you lead at this point?

2.

♠ 7
♡ A J 8 4
◇ 8 5 3
♣ A Q J 10 3

♠ A Q 8 5
♡ 7 2
◇ K 10 4
♣ 7 6 5 4

North opened 1♣, South responded 1♡, North raised to 2♡, South went to 4♡. You lead the ♠A, winning the first trick. Upon seeing dummy, what do you lead next?

3.

♠ 10 6 4 2
♡ J 8 5 3
◇ 5
♣ A J 6 4

♠ A K 5
♡ 10 9 7 4
◇ Q 10 7 3
♣ 8 3

South opened 1◇, North responded 1♡, South rebid 2♣, and all passed. You lead the ♠A, winning the first trick. What should you lead at trick two?

SOLUTIONS:

1. While your side may have tricks available in spades or clubs, there is no hurry to take them — dummy is now worthless, so how can declarer avoid any of his losers? Lead a diamond, forcing declarer to spend a trump (a trick he will always get anyway). By exiting safely, you give nothing away. Leading any other suit may cost a trick by giving declarer a "free finesse."

2. Here, dummy has teeth. Sooner or later, declarer will draw trumps, establish the clubs (if he doesn't have the ♣K), and discard his diamond losers. You can't afford to defend passively this time. Shift to a low diamond, hoping partner will produce the ace or at least the queen, allowing you to cash or establish some tricks before it's too late.

3.   Dummy has very little in high cards but does contain some trumps and a singleton diamond. Clearly, declarer can use dummy only by ruffing some diamonds, and you can tell he will need to do just that since your diamonds are fairly strong. Shift to a trump at trick two.

QUIZ ON DEFENSIVE SIGNALS:

I.   Partner has led the ♠4 against the opponents' contract of 3 NT. Dummy has A-8-5, and declarer plays the ace. What would you play from:

1. K93
2. 962
3. 987
4. Q106

II.   The opponents have reached a 4♠ contract, partner having over-called in hearts. Partner leads the ♡A and dummy tables:

♠ A J 3 2
♡ Q 8 5
◇ A 7 4
♣ K 5 3

What would you play from:

1. 107
2. KJ94
3. J952
4. 1074

REMEMBER YOUR DEFENSIVE SIGNALS — A HIGH CARD ENCOURAGES; A LOW CARD DISCOURAGES.

III.

♠ Q J 5 4
♡ A
◇ K 6 5
♣ J 9 7 5 3

♠ K 7
♡ K 10 8 5 2
◇ Q J 7
♣ 8 6 2

The opponents reached 3 NT and you led the ♡5. Declarer won in dummy and led a low spade to his 10. You won the king. What do you lead now if:

1. At trick one, partner played the nine and declarer played the three?
2. At trick one, partner played the three and declarer played the seven?

IV.

♠ K 6 4
♡ K 6 3
◇ 8 6 4 3
♣ Q 8 6

♠ 7
♡ A Q 9 8 4
◇ 9 5 2
♣ J 7 3 2

South opened 1 ♠, North raised to 2 ♠. South went on to 4 ♠. Your partner, West, led the ◇Q.

1. Which diamond do you play to trick one?
2. Which diamond would you play if you had nothing in hearts, but ◇K95?
3. Declarer wins the first trick with the ◇K and plays a trump to the king and a trump back toward his hand. What would you discard?

SOLUTIONS:

I.   1.   9   (encouraging)
     2.   2   (discouraging)
     3.   7   (discouraging)
     4.   10   (encouraging)
II.   1.   10   (encouraging, hoping to ruff the third heart)
     2.   9   (encouraging)
     3.   2   (discouraging)
     4.   4   (discouraging)
III.   1.   the ♡2
     2.   the ◊Q
IV.   1.   2   (discouraging)
     2.   9   (encouraging)
     3.   the ♡9, to show strength in that suit.

QUIZ ON RESPONDER'S REBID:

I.   *Opener*   *Responder*
    1 ◊   1 ♡
    2 ♣

1.   ♠ x x x   2.   ♠ x x x
    ♡ A Q x x   ♡ A Q x x
    ◊ x x   ◊ x x x x
    ♣ x x x x   ♣ x x

3.   ♠ x x x   4.   ♠ A x x x
    ♡ A Q x x x x   ♡ K Q x x x
    ◊ Q x   ◊ x
    ♣ x x   ♣ A x x

5.   ♠ K Q x x   6.   ♠ x x x
    ♡ A Q x x   ♡ A Q x x
    ◊ x x   ◊ x x
    ♣ x x x   ♣ K Q x x

7.   ♠ x x x   8.   ♠ x x
    ♡ A Q x x   ♡ K Q J x x x
    ◊ K Q x x   ◊ A x
    ♣ x x   ♣ J x x

9. ♠ K Q x
♥ A Q x x
♦ Q x x
♣ J x x

10. ♠ x x x
♥ A K x x
♦ x x
♣ A K J x

II. *Opener*   *Responder*
1 ♠   1 NT
2 ♦

1. ♠ x
♥ A Q x x
♦ J x x x
♣ x x x x

2. ♠ J x
♥ x x x x
♦ J x
♣ A Q x x x

3. ♠ x
♥ K Q 10 x x x
♦ J x
♣ J x x x

4. ♠ x
♥ A x x x
♦ K x x x x
♣ J x x

5. ♠ Q x
♥ Q 10 x x
♦ J x
♣ A 10 x x x

III. *Opener*   *Responder*
1 ♥   1 ♠
2 ♥

1. ♠ K Q x x
♥ x
♦ K x x x
♣ x x x x

2. ♠ A K x x x
♥ x x
♦ x x
♣ A K x x

3. ♠ A J x x x
♥ K Q x
♦ J x x x
♣ x

4. ♠ A K x x x
♥ x x
♦ x x x
♣ A K x

5. ♠ K 10 x x
♥ Q x
♦ K x x
♣ Q J x x

IV. *Opener* *Responder*
  1 ◇ 1 ♡
  1 NT

1. ♠ K Q x x
  ♡ A J x x
  ◇ K x x
  ♣ x x

2. ♠ K Q x x
  ♡ A J x x
  ◇ J x
  ♣ x x x

3. ♠ x
  ♡ K Q 10 x x x
  ◇ A x x
  ♣ J x x

4. ♠ x
  ♡ K Q J 10 x x
  ◇ A Q x
  ♣ x x x

5. ♠ A x x x
  ♡ K Q x x x
  ◇ ·A x
  ♣ x x

V. *Opener* *Responder*
  1 ◇ 1 ♠
  2 ♣

1. ♠ Q x x x
  ♡ x x x
  ◇ K x x x
  ♣ Q x

2. ♠ K Q x x
  ♡ A x x
  ◇ Q x
  ♣ x x x x

3. ♠ K Q x x x
  ♡ A x
  ◇ K x x
  ♣ x x x

4. ♠ J x x x
  ♡ A J x
  ◇ x x x
  ♣ A K x

VI. *Opener* *Responder*
  1 ♣ 1 ◇
  1 ♡

1. ♠ K J x
  ♡ x x
  ◇ Q x x x x
  ♣ J x x

2. ♠ x x x
  ♡ x
  ◇ A J x x x
  ♣ Q x x x

3. ♠ x x
   ♡ A J x x
   ◇ K Q x x x
   ♣ J x

4. ♠ K Q x
   ♡ J x
   ◇ A K x x x
   ♣ x x x

5. ♠ x x x
   ♡ x
   ◇ A K x x x
   ♣ K J x x

VII. Construct auctions for the following pairs of hands:

	Opener	*Responder*
1.	♠ K Q x	♠ A x x x
	♡ Q x	♡ J x x x
	◇ A J x x x	◇ K Q
	♣ Q x x	♣ J x x
2.	♠ A Q x x	♠ x x
	♡ x x	♡ A J x x x
	◇ A K x x	◇ Q x x x
	♣ x x x	♣ x x
3.	♠ x	♠ K Q J x x x
	♡ K x x	♡ A J x
	◇ A K x x x	◇ x x
	♣ Q J x x	♣ x x
4.	♠ x x	♠ A K x x
	♡ K x x	♡ A Q x x x
	◇ A K J x x x	◇ x x
	♣ Q x	♣ x x
5.	♠ x	♠ A Q J x x
	♡ K Q J x x x x	♡ x x
	◇ x x	◇ A K x
	♣ A J x	♣ x x x
6.	♠ A K x x	♠ x x x
	♡ x x	♡ K Q x x
	◇ A K 10 x x	◇ Q x
	♣ K x	♣ Q 10 x x

107

SOLUTIONS:

I.
1. Pass
2. 2♦
3. 2♥
4. 2♠
5. 2 NT
6. 3♣
7. 3♦
8. 3♥
9. 3 NT
10. 4♣ or 5♣

II.
1. Pass
2. 2♠
3. 2♥
4. 3♦
5. 2 NT

III.
1. Pass
2. 3♣
3. 4♥
4. 3♣. Invent a suit to temporize.
5. 2 NT

IV.
1. 3 NT
2. 2 NT
3. 3♥
4. 4♥
5. 2♠

V.
1. Pass
2. 3♠
3. 4♠
4. 3 NT

VI.
1. 1 NT
2. 2♣
3. 3♥
4. 3 NT
5. 3♣

VII.
1. 1♦ - 1♥
1 NT - 2 NT
3 NT - Pass

2. 1♦ - 1♥
1♠ - 2♦
Pass

3. 1♦ - 1♠
2♣ - 3♠
Pass

4. 1♦ - 1♥
2♦ - 2♠
3♥ - 4♥
Pass

5. 1♥ - 1♠
2♥ - 3♦
3♥ - 4♥
Pass

6. 1♦ - 1♥
1♠ - 1 NT
2 NT - 3 NT
Pass

Chapter 7

THINKING:
DEFENSE — CHOOSING YOUR OPENING LEAD
SLAM BIDDING THE EXPERT WAY

THINKING: DEFENSE — CHOOSING YOUR OPENING LEAD

Defense is probably the toughest part of bridge, and opening leads are, in turn, the most troublesome part of defense. Nevertheless, opening leads are by no means all guesswork. By listening to the bidding, looking at your own hand, and using a little imagination, it is possible to produce effective opening leads consistently. In this chapter, we will see how a good player's thought processes work when he selects an opening lead.

To begin, let's look again at a hand from the last chapter.

1.
        ♠ 9 7 5 3 2
        ♡ K 6 5 3
        ◇ A 9 8
        ♣ 4

♠ A K 10 8
♡ Q 10 9 8
◇ 7 5 2
♣ J 7

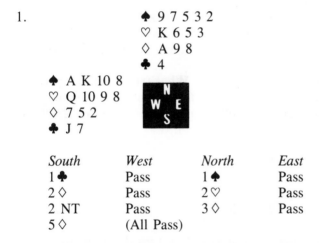

South	West	North	East
1 ♣	Pass	1 ♠	Pass
2 ◇	Pass	2 ♡	Pass
2 NT	Pass	3 ◇	Pass
5 ◇	(All Pass)		

You, West, led the ♠ A against the 5 ◇ contract, winning the first trick as declarer dropped the jack. Next, you shifted to a *trump*, imagining that declarer would try to make use of dummy by *ruffing* his losing clubs. Your play was a success, since declarer's hand was:

♠ J
♡ A 7 2
◇ K Q J 6
♣ A K 9 6 3

But wait a minute. Didn't the *auction suggest* that declarer would ruff losers in dummy? Didn't dummy show a moderate hand with spades and hearts, plus diamond support; therefore, very short in clubs? *You should have led a trump on opening lead!* You knew, since you had a stout holding in both spades and hearts, that dummy would produce few tricks in those suits. But the danger of ruffing potential in dummy was obvious, *if* you *listened* to the opponents' bidding.

How would you imagine the play will go on this hand?

South	West	North	East
			1 ♠
Pass	2 ◇	Pass	2 ♠
Pass	4 ♠	(All Pass)	

Dummy will put down a fairly strong hand here. East's 2 ♠ rebid showed a minimum opening, but West went straight to a game anyway. There will be spade support; and a diamond suit, maybe a good one.

How will declarer use dummy? What tricks will it provide? Most likely, declarer will try to set up the dummy's diamonds and throw away his losers in the other suits. Suppose you are South, to make the opening lead from this hand:

2. ♠ 7 5 3
    ♡ K J 5 3
    ◇ Q 7 5
    ♣ J 9 3

Will declarer succeed if he tries to set up the diamonds? The diamond suit *will* come in, from your point of view. Your ◇ Q is badly placed in front of dummy's suit. If declarer wants to take a finesse to dummy's ◇ AKJxx, it will work like a charm. His losers in hearts and clubs will go away.

You must get busy and get some tricks in a hurry, even if it means taking a chance. (Remember the hand from the *last* chapter when it was necessary to lead a heart into dummy's ace-jack, desperately hoping that partner had the queen?) The most aggressive lead you can make is a low heart. If partner has the ♡A, you may take two or three fast tricks. If he has the ♡Q, you may establish a trick or two right away. Fast tricks will be required to beat this contract. The opponents' bidding and your own hand clearly indicate it.

Many textbooks begin a discussion of opening leads by supplying a list of the most attractive holdings to lead from. Chief among them are an ace-king combination; any sequential holding; a suit partner has bid; and a singleton. Making an intelligent opening lead really asks more of you than to look at a table. You must *use your imagination and visualize how declarer intends to use dummy's values.* Then you can plan what your *strategy* will be to *counter* his plans.

In our first example, we saw that even an ace-king combination may not be your best lead. The same goes for leading your partner's suit.

South	West	North	East
			1 ◇
Pass	1 ♡	1 ♠	1 NT
Pass	2 ◇	(All Pass)	

You are South and must lead from this hand:

3.
    ♠ 10 4
    ♡ Q 10 9 7
    ◇ 7 5 3
    ♣ A J 9 3

What sort of hand will dummy put down? Weak or strong? Weak, judging by his bidding. **Balanced or unbalanced?** Surely unbalanced, since he preferred to play in partner's suit and not in notrump. A likely hand for dummy is:

    ♠ 6 5
    ♡ A J 6 2
    ◇ Q 9 6 2
    ♣ 8 5 2

What is dummy's source of tricks? Right, *ruffing* tricks. Not heart or club tricks, since you have a good holding in each of those suits. So you should lead a trump, in spite of partner's bid.

How about this situation?

South	West	North	East
		.	1 ♠
Pass	2 ♠	(All Pass)	

You are South and must lead from this hand:

4. ♠ Q 8 5
    ♡ 6 3
    ◇ Q J 10 4
    ♣ A 10 7 3

Here, you *should* follow the textbook advice and lead your ◇ Q. The dummy will be weak and declarer will have trouble in the play when he has limited help in dummy. Make your normal, passive lead from your sequence, and *wait* to see what happens. Contrast this situation with the second hand, where snatching fast tricks was a necessity.

In discussing defensive strategy, we said that the defenders' best hope of tricks vs. notrump is the establishment of some *long* cards. So you will usually apply the "fourth-from-your-longest-and-strongest" approach in making your opening lead against a notrump contract. If your hand is very weak, and your suit is poor, however, think twice.

South	West	North	East
			1 NT
Pass	3 NT	(All Pass)	

5. ♠ 10 7 5 2
    ♡ J 10
    ◇ J 9 5 4 2
    ♣ 8 5

What should you lead as South?
A diamond lead is unlikely to accomplish anything. Even if you get your long cards set up, you have no entry to cash them. But your partner is marked with some entries. (If he had no high cards, the enemy would have bid a slam instead of stopping in game.) Perhaps you should try to set up *his* suit. **Which suit is he likely to have length in?** Since the opponents made no effort to reach a major-suit game (West could have used the Stayman Convention with four cards

in hearts or spades), partner is almost sure to have *at least four* hearts, and perhaps more. So leading your ♡J is best.

Let's look at one more common situation. You love to lead *singletons,* we'll bet. The lead of a singleton (or small doubleton) can be very effective, but other times it may be a disaster. The suit you are short in may be declarer's *best* suit. You may help him *establish* it and present him with some *timing* on the hand as well. Do not lead from shortness unless there is a fair chance your lead will work. Look at this problem.

South	West	North	East
			1 ♠
Pass	3 ♠	Pass	4 ♠
(All Pass)			

You are South and must lead from this hand:

6.
♠ J 4 2
♡ A Q 7 6 4
◊ K Q 10 3
♣ 3

Would you lead your singleton club?

For you to get a club ruff on this hand, partner will have to gain the lead at some point. **How likely is this?** On the opponents' bidding, partner holds only a queen at most. If you expect him to have the ♣A, you're really living in a dream world! (He might have the ♣Q, in which case he won't appreciate your lead very much.)

Leading your singleton in this situation is much more likely to cost a trick than to gain one. *Your hand is too strong.* A lead from the top of your diamond sequence is more realistic.

If your hand were:

7.
♠ A 7 5
♡ J 9 6 4 2
◊ 8 6 5 2
♣ 3

the singleton-club lead would be odds-on to work. You have a weak hand, so you can hypothetically put some high cards in your partner's hand as entries. He might well have the ♣A! Also, you have an important card, the *ace of trumps.* This means that *declarer can-*

113

not draw trumps without letting you regain the lead. Your chances of getting a club ruff are assured if partner has *any* fast entry.

SLAM BIDDING THE EXPERT WAY

To make a small slam, you must have the material for 12 tricks *and* you must be able to prevent the defenders, who get to make the opening lead, from cashing two *fast* tricks to beat you. Your trick-taking POWER may come from great *high-card* strength, or from a big trump *fit*, plus good *distribution*. For your CONTROLS, you need all the *aces*, or at least three of the aces, plus a king in the fourth suit. (Voids and singletons may do as well in a suit contract.)

The easiest slams to bid are those based on sheer POWER. Partner opens 1 NT and you have:

♠ A x x
♡ K x x
◇ A Q x x
♣ K J x

You know there are at least 33 high-card points in the combined hands, so you can just bid 6 NT.

You open 1♠ on:

♠ A K 9 6 4
♡ A 8 6
◇ A J 5
♣ K 6

Partner responds 3♠. Your hand is worth about 20 points and partner showed 13-15. So you have the values for slam, and can bid 6♠ directly. Notice that in each of these examples, CONTROLS are no problem. (In the first example, it is impossible for the opponents to have two aces and unlikely that they have an ace-king in the same suit when your side has 33 high-card points.)

Direct auctions like these have an advantage. The opponents have little information on which to base their opening lead and later defense. But *too much speculation* in bidding slams is a bad idea. You have a lot to lose (a game bonus) by going down at slam; so we often prefer a go-slow approach, hoping to find out if the elements that make a good slam are present.

114

Suppose you have enough POWER for a slam contract, but you are worried about CONTROLS. The BLACKWOOD CONVENTION *may* solve your problems. A bid of *4 NT* is often* used to ask partner *how many* aces he holds. The responses:

With no aces	5 ♣
With 1 ace	5 ◊
With 2 aces	5 ♡
With 3 aces	5 ♠
With 4 aces	5 ♣

Note that the response for four aces and no aces is the same. Presumably, the player who uses Blackwood will be able to tell by looking at his own hand. IF YOUR SIDE HAS ALL THE ACES, you may continue with a bid of *5NT,* which asks for *kings* AND IMPLIES INTEREST IN A GRAND SLAM.

Suppose that your hand is:

> ♠ K Q 8 6 5
> ♡ K Q J 7 5
> ◊ A K
> ♣ 5

You open 1 ♠ and partner responds 3 ♠. BLACKWOOD is *perfect.* You can place the contract if you know just one piece of information, partner's aces. If he responds 5 ◊, you *sign off* at 5 ♠. If he says 5 ♡, you bid 6 ♠. If he responds 5 ♠, you bid a grand slam.

Unfortunately, *not every hand is so well-suited to BLACKWOOD.* Not many players believe this, however, because Blackwood is the most abused of all conventions. People persist in using Blackwood *when it will not tell them what they need to know.* We have, after all, seen that slams depend on more than just aces.

———

*4 NT is merely a *raise* in notrump, showing general slam interest, when bid over a notrump opening or response. It should *not* be Blackwood unless a trump suit is agreed on, if only by implication.

115

For example, you hold this hand:

♠ K 9 6 5 2
♡ —
◊ A K 5
♣ K J 7 6 3

You open 1♣ and partner responds 3♣. Blackwood is useless. For slam to be a good bet, partner needs *specific* aces (the ♡*A* would be of little use), while Blackwood will only tell you *how many* aces he has. (You also need *good* trumps from partner, plus help in *clubs*, and Blackwood is no help there either. A worse hand to use Blackwood could hardly be constructed; but a lot of players believe that you aren't allowed to bid slam unless you use Blackwood first.) How about this hand?

♠ K Q 9 5 3
♡ A J 4
◊ A 8 6
♣ K 6

Partner replies 3♠ to your 1♠ opening. You have several *losers* on this hand. You need to know if partner has a maximum 3♠ response, so he can provide extra help for your losers. You are worried about the lack of POWER here. Blackwood won't help.

The biggest drawback to indiscriminate use of Blackwood is shown here. Your hand is:

♠ A Q J 6 4
♡ 7 5
◊ K 3
♣ A Q J 4

You open 1♠, partner replies 3♠. Suppose you use Blackwood (an error, as we will see), and partner shows *one* ace. The danger in bidding slam is that you might be off the ♡*A and the* ♡*K as well.* No CONTROL in that suit.

116

Note this well:

THE TIME TO USE BLACKWOOD IS WHEN YOU KNOW THE POWER, GOOD TRUMPS AND CONTROLS FOR SLAM ARE AVAILABLE, AND THE ONLY WORRY IS THAT TWO ACES MAY BE MISSING. BLACKWOOD WAS INTENDED NOT AS A SLAM-BIDDING TOOL, BUT AS A WAY TO AVOID SLAM WITH A LACK OF ACES.

The element of CONTROLS is so important, in fact, that one alternative method of slam bidding is based on showing CONTROLS. This method, called CUEBIDDING, is favored by better players.

CUEBIDDING AS A SLAM-BIDDING METHOD:

Perhaps you have already heard of CUEBIDS in a different context, as *a bid of the opponents' suit.* If you were about to open with a strong two-bid, and your right-hand opponent surprises you by opening the bidding, you CUEBID his suit. This direct CUEBID tells partner not to be intimidated by the opposing opening — you promise a game in your own hand, ample playing strength and good defense.

The CUEBID we will look at here is different:

ONCE A TRUMP SUIT IS AGREED ON, A BID OF *ANOTHER* SUIT AT THE LEVEL OF GAME OR HIGHER SHOWS INTEREST IN SLAM AND *PROMISES A CONTROL* (most often the ace, sometimes the king or shortness) IN THE BID SUIT. PARTNER IS INVITED TO BID A SLAM OR RETURN THE INTEREST BY CUEBIDDING A SUIT IN WHICH *HE* HOLDS A CONTROL. AFTER ONE OR MORE CUEBIDS, THE PARTNERSHIP MAY OR MAY NOT DECIDE THAT THEY HAVE THE POWER AND CONTROLS FOR A SLAM.

Let's use our last example hand as an illustration, with a possible hand for responder added.

Opener	Responder
♠ A Q J 6 4	♠ K 9 5 2
♡ 7 5	♡ Q 8 2
◊ K 3	◊ A J 7 4
♣ A Q J 4	♣ K 5

1 ♠	3 ♠
4 ♣ (1)	4 ◊ (2)
4 ♠ (3)	5 ♣ (4)
5 ◊ (5)	5 ♠ (6)
Pass (7)	

(1) "I have a club control, probably the *ace,* and I think we may have a slam."
(2) "I have a diamond control, probably the *ace,* and you might be right."
(3) "I don't have the ♡ A to show you, and my slam interest was only mild anyway. I'll leave any further move up to you."
(4) "I can't bid a slam, but I do have the ♣ K (*second*-round control) in case you're interested."
(5) "I still can't go to six, but I have the ◊ K. Can you bid slam now?"
(6) "I have no heart control."
(7) "Looks as if we have two heart losers."

Notice how eloquent a conversation the partnership can carry on. Let's give responder an alternative hand, with slam a laydown.

Opener	Responder
♠ A Q J 6 4	♠ K 9 5 2
♡ 7 5	♡ A 8 2
◊ K 3	◊ Q J 7 4
♣ A Q J 4	♣ K 5
1 ♠	3 ♠
4 ♣ (1)	4 ♡ (2)
4 ♠ (3)	5 ♣ (4)
6 ♠ (5)	Pass

(1) "I have a club control, probably the ace, and I'm interested."
(2) "I have a heart control, probably the ace, and I'm also interested."
(3) In theory, opener could take over with BLACKWOOD here, since he now knows that all the suits are under control. Instead, he says that his slam interest is only mild and leaves the next move up to responder.
(4) "I have the ♣K, in case you want to know."
(5) "I have a diamond control and the prospects of ample tricks, so I can bid a slam."

NOTICE THAT RESPONDER WOULD SHOW ONE ACE IN REPLY TO BLACKWOOD ON *BOTH* THESE HANDS.

CUEBIDDING to slam is often a *superior* method to Blackwood for several reasons:

---

1. It is more *flexible*. Either partner may use his judgment at any time and bid a slam. In Blackwood, the 4 NT bidder must make all the decisions for his partnership.
2. The partnership can show *where* its values are located.
3. It is possible to show your interest in slam without going as *high* as 4 NT.

Remember, however, that you *cannot* begin CUEBIDDING while the trump suit is still in doubt, or when it is not clear that your side is even in the slam zone. In this auction:

Opener	Responder
1 ◇	2 ◇
2 ♠	

opener is still trying to suggest the *major* suit as trumps. And here:

Opener	Responder
1 ♠	2 ♠
3 ♡	

opener may be only trying for *game* if responder has a good raise or a good holding in hearts as well as spades.

The *first* cuebid you make, as we have seen, normally shows a *first*-round control, an ace (rarely, a void suit). A further cuebid of this same suit by either partner, therefore, would suggest *second*-round control, the king (rarely, a singleton.)

Let's look at some other auctions that illustrate cuebidding:

Opener	Responder
♠ A K 6 4	♠ 8 3
♡ K 7 4	♡ A Q J 10 5
◇ Q 6	◇ A K 7 5
♣ A 8 5 4	♣ 7 2
1 NT	3 ♡ (1)
4 ♡	5 ◇ (2)
6 ♡ (3)	Pass

(1) Ten or more points, five or more good hearts, forcing to game.
(2) Slam interest, diamond control, probably the ace.
(3) Good hand for slam, with a heart honor, a diamond honor, and top tricks in the black suits.

Opener	Responder
♠ K J 5	♠ A Q 9 7 4 2
♡ A K J 4	♡ 6
◇ Q 7 6 4	◇ J 2
♣ Q 7	♣ A K 6 2

1 NT	3 ♠
4 ♠	5 ♣ (1)
5 ♡ (2)	5 ♠ (3)
Pass (4)	

(1) Club control, slam interest.
(2) Heart control, returning the interest.
(3) "I can't bid slam without a diamond control."
(4) "Neither can I."

On rare occasions you may cuebid when a trump suit has been agreed on, only by *implication*.
You hold this hand:

♠ —
♡ K Q 8 6 5
◇ A 8 5 3
♣ K J 8 5

Partner opens 1 ♡ and right-hand opponent overcalls 1 ♠. You should bid 2 ♠. This cuebid implies tremendous support for partner's suit (since you failed to suggest a suit of your own) a control in spades (frequently a *void*), and interest in slam (since you could have merely raised hearts if interested only in game).
You hold this hand:

♠ A Q 6 4
♡ K 10 4
◇ 6 4
♣ A K J 4

Partner responds 3 ♠ to your 1 NT opening. Your rebid should be 4 ♣. Partner asked you to choose between spades and notrump. You would return to 3 NT with no support for his suit, so your 4 ♣ must agree with spades. Furthermore, since you would just raise to 4 ♠ with most hands, 4 ♣ must show a really excellent hand with

121

fine spade support. You make this bid (called an "advance" cuebid) in case partner is strong enough to consider slam. You can *save some space* in the bidding.

Opener	*Responder*
♠ A Q 6 4	♠ K J 9 7 3
♡ K 10 4	♡ Q 6
◊ 6 4	◊ A K 8 5
♣ A K J 4	♣ 7 3
1 NT	3 ♠
4 ♣ (1)	4 ◊ (2)
4 ♠ (3)	5 ◊ (4)
6 ♠ (5)	Pass

(1) Club control, slam interest, spades agreed by implication.
(2) Diamond control, slam interest.
(3) "I can't make any aggressive move at this point."
(4) *Second*-round diamond control, still interested.
(5) "I have a heart control, so I'll take a chance."

TEST YOUR COMPREHENSION OF THE MATERIAL IN THIS CHAPTER:

QUIZ ON CHOOSING YOUR OPENING LEAD:

The bidding has been:

1.
South	West	North	East
	1♠	Pass	2♡
Pass	3♡	Pass	4♡
(All Pass)			

Your hand, as South:

♠ Q 5 4
♡ 8 6 4
◊ K J 5
♣ J 9 6 4

2.
South	West	North	East
			1♠
Pass	2♠	(All Pass)	

♠ 8 5 3
♡ Q 9 5 3
◊ K 8 4
♣ J 9 3

3.
South	West	North	East
			1♠
Pass	3♠	Pass	4♠
(All Pass)			

♠ J 6 4
♡ Q J 10 4 3
◊ A 8
♣ K 6 4

123

4.

South	West	North	East
			1 ♥
Pass	1 ♠	Pass	2 ♥
(All Pass)			

♠ 7 5 3
♡ K Q 4
◇ K 5 3
♣ Q 9 5 3

5.

South	West	North	East
			1 ◇
Pass	1 ♡	Pass	2 ♣
(All Pass)			

♠ K Q 6 4
♡ J 6 4
◇ A J 9 4
♣ 9 7

6.

South	West	North	East
			1 NT
Pass	3 NT	(All Pass)	

♠ A K 7 5 3
♡ 8 6 4
◇ J 4
♣ 6 5 3

7.

South	West	North	East
			1 ◇
Pass	1 ♡	1 ♠	2 ◇
Pass	3 ◇	Pass	3 NT
(All Pass)			

♠ 9 4
♡ Q 7 4
◇ 7 6 5
♣ Q 10 7 5 2

8. | South | West | North | East |
|---|---|---|---|
| | | | 1 NT |
| Pass | 3 NT | (All Pass) | |

    ♠ 10 9 4
    ♡ J 8 6 4
    ◊ 10 8 6 4 2
    ♣ 8

9. | South | West | North | East |
|---|---|---|---|
| | | | 1 NT |
| Pass | 2 ♣ | Pass | 2 ♠ |
| Pass | 4 ♠ | (All Pass) | |

    ♠ A 7 5
    ♡ K Q 10 4
    ◊ A 9 7 5 3
    ♣ 5

10. | South | West | North | East |
|---|---|---|---|
| | | | 1 ♡ |
| Pass | 4 ♡ | (All Pass) | |

    ♠ J 10 9 6 4
    ♡ A 7 5
    ◊ 5
    ♣ 10 6 4 2

SUCCESSFUL LEADS AGAINST SUIT CONTRACTS REQUIRE CAREFUL THOUGHT AND A LITTLE LUCK.

SOLUTIONS:

1. ◊ 5, hoping to get a *fast trick* or two before declarer establishes the spades for discards.
2. ♠ 3. Play *safe,* with dummy known to be weak.
3. ♡ Q, the normal *top-of-sequence* lead. This lead combines safety with a try at building a trick. Your hand is too strong to lay down the ◊ A. Partner is most unlikely to have the king.
4. ♠ 7. A *passive* lead, with dummy known to be weak.
5. ♣ 7. Dummy's most likely source of tricks is ruffing power on this auction, and you can tell declarer has losing diamonds to ruff since yours are strong.
6. ♠ 5. You must lead *low* here to keep communication with partner's hand, since you have no sure entry.
7. ♠ 9. *Lead your partner's suit.* He is likely to have a good suit for his overcall, plus entries.
8. ♠ 10, hoping to *find partner's long suit.*
9. ♡ K. You are too strong to lead your singleton club. Partner will probably never win a trick on this hand.
10. ◊ 5. You have a weak hand, so partner probably has an entry somewhere. Plus, you have trump control.

QUIZ ON SLAM BIDDING THE EXPERT WAY:

1. Partner opens 1 NT. What is your response with:

   ♠ A Q x
   ♡ K x x
   ◊ A Q x x x
   ♣ Q x

2. You open 1 ♠, partner responds 3 ♠. What is your rebid with:

   (a) ♠ A Q x x x
   ♡ A J x x
   ◊ A x
   ♣ K x

   (b) ♠ K Q J x x x
   ♡ K Q x x
   ◊ x
   ♣ A x

   (c) ♠ A Q x x x
   ♡ x x
   ◊ K x
   ♣ A K J x

   (d) ♠ K J x x x
   ♡ x
   ◊ A K J x x
   ♣ x x

3. You open 1 ♠, partner responds 3 ♠. With which of these hands would you now employ the Blackwood Convention?

(a)   ♠ A J x x x   (b)   ♠ J x x x x
      ♡ K x x   ♡ A K Q x
      ◊ A x x   ◊ A Q x
      ♣ A x   ♣ x

(c)   ♠ A K x x x x   (d)   ♠ A Q x x x
      ♡ x   ♡ A K
      ◊ A K J x   ◊ x x x
      ♣ K x   ♣ A x x

(e)   ♠ A K x x x
      ♡ A J x x
      ◊ —
      ♣ K J x x

4. You open 1 ♠, partner responds 3 ♠. What is your rebid with:

(a)   ♠ A J x x x   (b)   ♠ K Q x x x
      ♡ Q J x   ♡ x x
      ◊ K x x   ◊ A Q J x x
      ♣ A x   ♣ x

(c)   ♠ A Q x x x
      ♡ x x x
      ◊ A Q x
      ♣ A x

5. Partner opened 1 ♠, you responded 3 ♠, he bid 4 ♣. What do you bid now with:

(a)   ♠ K Q x x   (b)   ♠ K J x x
      ♡ x x x   ♡ A x x
      ◊ A Q x x   ◊ K J x
      ♣ K x   ♣ J x x

6. Construct auctions for the following pairs of hands, using *cuebids* to reach a good slam or avoid a bad one.

	Opener	*Responder*
(a)	♠ Q x x x	♠ A K J x x
	♡ A x x x	♡ x
	◊ x x	◊ A K Q J x
	♣ A J x	♣ x x
(b)	♠ K x	♠ A Q x x
	♡ A J 10 x x	♡ K Q x x
	◊ J x x	◊ Q x
	♣ A K x	♣ x x x
(c)	♠ K Q 10 x x	♠ A x
	♡ A x	♡ x x
	◊ J x	◊ A Q x
	♣ A Q x x	♣ K J x x x x
(d)	♠ x x	♠ A x
	♡ Q x x	♡ A K J x x x x
	◊ A Q x	◊ x x
	♣ A Q x x x	♣ K x

SOLUTIONS:

1. 6 NT
2a. 6♠
  b. 4 NT
  c. 4♣
  d. 4♠. No point in bidding 4◊, which would be a *cuebid*.
3a. Only (c) is suitable for a Blackwood bid. With (a), you must be concerned about sufficient *power* for slam. With (b) the problem is a shaky *trump* holding. With (d), you have no *control* in diamonds. With (e), you have a void suit and need to know about *specific* aces.
4a. 4♠
  b. 4♠
  c. 4♣ or 4◊
5a. 4◊
  b. 4♠. Do not encourage slam by cuebidding the ♡A. Your hand is terrible.

6a. *Opener*   *Responder*
     Pass   1♠
     3♠   4◊ (1)
     4♡ (2)   5♠ (3)
     6♣ (4)   7♠

(1) Control, slam interest.
(2) Control, slam interest.
(3) Clubs is the *only* problem.
(4) First-round club control.

6b. *Opener*   *Responder*
     1♡   3♡
     4♣ (1)   4♡ (2)
     Pass (3)

(1) Control, slam interest.
(2) I have a bad hand and I'm not willing to go past game to show the ♠A.
(3) I give up.

6c. *Opener*   *Responder*
     1♠   2♣
     4♣   4◊ (1)
     4♡ (1)   4♠ (1)
     6♣ (2)   7♣ (3)

(1) Controls, slam interest.
(2) I'm willing.
(3) I have an *extra* club winner, so I'll shoot the moon.

6d. *Opener*   *Responder*
     1♣   2♡
     3♡   3♠ (1)
     4♣ (1)   4♡ (2)
     5◊ (1)   7♡ (3)

(1) Controls, slam interest.
(2) I can't do any more with nothing in diamonds.
(3) It looks as if we have 'em all.

Chapter 8

THINKING: DEFENSE —
RECONSTRUCTING DECLARER'S HAND
BALANCING

THINKING: DEFENSE —
RECONSTRUCTING DECLARER'S HAND

A few chapters ago, we talked about reconstructing the opponents' *distribution* and *high-card points* as declarer. While this is a useful technique, it is not required on every hand. *But if you are a defender, you must always try to figure out what declarer has.* Otherwise, it is impossible to produce the best defense consistently.

The defenders operate under the handicap of not seeing each other's hands. Good defense requires deductive reasoning. Trying to reconstruct declarer's *distribution* and *high-card structure* is part of this reasoning. Let's look at a simple example:

1.
                       ♠ Q 9
                       ♡ K 6
                       ◇ K 10 7 2
                       ♣ A K J 5 4

   ♠ K J 7 2
   ♡ J 10 9 4   N
   ◇ Q 6 3   W   E
   ♣ 10 6   S

The bidding:

South	West	North	East
Pass	Pass	1 ♣	Pass
1 ◇	Pass	3 ◇	Pass
4 ◇	Pass	5 ◇	(All Pass)

You, West, lead the ♡J. Dummy's king wins and declarer leads the ◇2 to his jack and your queen. **What should you lead now?**

A simple count of declarer's *points* will guide you. He is known to have the ♡A and the ◇A and ◇J, from the play so far. *East* has the ♠ A, therefore. If declarer had it, he would not have passed as dealer. If declarer's hand is:

♠ 10 4
♡ A 8 7 2
◇ A J 8 4
♣ Q 9 3

you must lead a spade and get your tricks right away, before declarer draws trumps and runs dummy's clubs for discards.

Counting declarer's *distribution* is an equally important job. The *bidding* will often give you a rough idea of declarer's pattern. For example, if the bidding goes:

Opener	Responder
1 ♠	2 ◇
2 ♡	2 NT
3 ♠	

you can expect opener to have six spades and four hearts. In the play, you note the opening lead and see declarer show out as suits are led. Pretty soon, you may know his distribution completely. Look at this hand:

2.

♠ A 7 6 5 2
♡ 6 5
◇ K 9
♣ K J 9 4

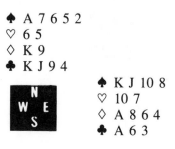

♠ K J 10 8
♡ 10 7
◇ A 8 6 4
♣ A 6 3

The bidding:

South	West	North	East
1 ♡	Pass	1 ♠	Pass
2 ♣	Pass	3 ♣	Pass
3 NT	(All Pass)		

West leads the ◇ 2 and you win dummy's nine with the ace. **Should you return partner's lead automatically?**

131

Before doing *anything*, try to count declarer's pattern. He showed a heart suit and a club suit. **How many cards would you expect him to have in each one?** Four cards in each suit? No, he would have opened *1♣*. Six hearts? No, he would have rebid hearts at some point. Five hearts and five clubs? No, he would probably have preferred to play game in clubs with that unbalanced hand. Most likely, declarer has *five* hearts and *four* clubs.

Now, how many diamonds does declarer have? **What does the opening lead tell you?** Partner's ◇2 suggests a *four*-card suit, so declarer has *three* diamonds. **What do you think declarer has in diamonds?** Surely he has some high card. He did, after all, bid 3 NT before he knew the ◇K would be in dummy. He would have to be a madman to bid it with nothing good in diamonds.

How many spades does declarer have? One spade. **What is the best defense at this point?** Shift to the ♠*K*. The king should be led in case declarer's singleton is the queen. You will establish three spade tricks that you can cash when you get in with the ♣A. On this hand, a count of declarer's distribution will let you avoid the "automatic" return of partner's lead.

3.
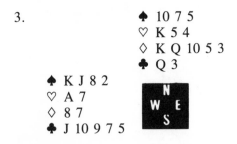

    ♠ 10 7 5
    ♡ K 5 4
    ◇ K Q 10 5 3
    ♣ Q 3

♠ K J 8 2
♡ A 7
◇ 8 7
♣ J 10 9 7 5

South opened 1 NT (16-18 HCP) and North raised to 3 NT. You, West, lead the ♣J. Declarer plays dummy's ♣Q, which wins. His next play is a heart from dummy to his queen, and you win the ace. **What should you do now?**

Let's see if you can figure out what declarer has for his 1 NT opening. **What does he have in clubs?** He must have the ace and king, since partner would have played one of those cards at trick one. Declarer also has the ♡Q, so that's 9 of his points you know about.

How about the diamond suit? **Who do you think has good diamonds?** Put yourself in declarer's place. Suppose *you* were declarer, and your diamond holding were J-x-x or three or four small cards. *How would you play this hand?* What suit would you establish immediately? *Diamonds,* of course. Why isn't declarer establishing his best suit? It must already be established! Any time dummy has a nice-looking suit and declarer leads some *other* suit, chances are he can cash dummy's best suit whenever he feels like it. So it is almost certain that declarer has the ◊ A (and maybe the jack as well).

Inferring that declarer has the ◊ A, you know about *13* of his high-card points. **So, how good are declarer's spades?** They can't be as good as ace-queen, can they? That would give him 19 high-card points, too many for his 1 NT opening.

So a shift to the ♠2 cannot cost since partner must have *one* honor. And it is really the only chance for the defense. Count declarer's *tricks*. He has three in clubs, you expect the diamond suit to produce five tricks for him, and the ♡K is now a winner. That's nine tricks. The contract will be made unless you lead a spade right now and find partner with the ace.

Perhaps declarer's hand is:

♠ Q 4
♡ Q 9 2
◊ A J 9 4
♣ A K 6 2

and you will get five tricks on a spade switch and return before declarer can take his tricks. Notice that declarer's play of leading a heart immediately, trying for his ninth trick, made the defense of this contract tougher.

On this hand, you counted declarer's high-card *points* and his certain *tricks*. Also, you drew an *inference* from the way he handled the play in order to reconstruct his holding and choose the best defense.

BALANCING

So far in our review of bidding skills, we have dealt strictly with *constructive auctions*. In real life, you will have opponents at the table, and many auctions will be *competitive*. *Both* sides may have a share of the high-card strength and/or a good suit. Accuracy in competitive bidding is the lifeblood of success at bridge.

You should be familiar with your possible actions when the bidding is opened by your right-hand opponent: the *overcall*, the *jump overcall*, the *preempt*, the *1 NT overcall*, the *takeout double*, the *cuebid*, and finally, but by no means the least important, *pass*. There are many possible benefits from entering the opponents' auction, but there are obvious dangers as well.

In this chapter, we will discuss entering the auction even though the opponents have made the first bid. We will also talk about *how high* you should compete if the auction turns competitive.

First, let's examine an important concept called "balancing."

> WHEN THE OPPONENTS STOP BIDDING AT A LOW LEVEL, AND ESPECIALLY WHEN THEY FIND A GOOD TRUMP SUIT, YOU SHOULD CONSIDER BACKING INTO THE AUCTION EVEN IF YOU WERE NOT STRONG ENOUGH TO TAKE ANY DIRECT ACTION BEFORE.

A "balancing" action is often very *safe;* your side must have a share of the high-card strength when the opponents stop low; and the fact that they have a trump suit makes it likely that your side has one also.

> IT IS LOSING TACTICS TO LET THE OPPONENTS PLAY COMFORTABLY AT THE ONE OR TWO LEVEL. A BALANCING BID OR (TAKEOUT) DOUBLE BY YOU MAY GET YOUR SIDE TO A MAKABLE CONTRACT OR DRIVE THE OPPONENTS UP TO A LEVEL WHERE YOU CAN SET THEM.

Look at this situation:

East	South	West	North
1 ♡	Pass	2 ♡	Pass
Pass	?		

You, South, must choose an action with:

1. ♠ Q J x x x
   ♡ x x
   ◊ K x x
   ♣ Q x x

You weren't strong enough to overcall 1 ♠ immediately, but now it is correct to *balance* with *2 ♠*.

The opponents have shown no interest in game, so they have at most 23 high-card points and might have as few as 19 or 20. Partner, therefore, is marked with some values, perhaps as much as an opening bid! (Why didn't North act over 2 ♡ if his hand was worth opening? With a *defensively*-oriented hand containing scattered points, especially points in the *opponents'* suit, but *lacking tricks,* he might choose to wait.) It is, in fact, safer to bid 2♠ now than it would have been to overcall at your first turn. And you may drive the opponents to *3♡*, where your chances for a plus score will be greater; or you may make 2♠, if they let you play it.

East	South	West	North
1 ♡	Pass	2 ♡	Pass
Pass	?		

2. ♠ A x
    ♡ A x x x
    ◊ K J 10 x x
    ♣ x x

Bid 3 ◊. A 2 ◊ overcall would have been dangerous, but this is relatively safe.

3. ♠ K J 10 x
    ♡ A x x x
    ◊ J x x
    ♣ x x

2♠. You would rather have five spades. However, partner is short in hearts, so he probably has some spade length.

4. ♠ K x x x
    ♡ x x
    ◊ A x x x
    ♣ Q x x

Double. This double is *for takeout* (even though it is not your first turn to double a heart bid). When the opponents stop low and you *reopen* the bidding with a balancing double, your double is *not* for penalties. This is an *exception* to the rules about doubles for penalty vs. takeout.

5. ♠ x x x
    ♡ Q J x
    ◊ K x x x
    ♣ K x x

This time you must pass. You have more than enough points to balance, but your points are the wrong ones. The ♡Q and ♡J will be worthless to your side if you declare, and since you possess those cards, your chances of finding partner with some values that *will* be useful are decreased. It is too *dangerous* to balance.

6. ♠ x   Bid 2 NT. This is a *conventional* bid. You
   ♡ A x   couldn't want to bid 2 NT to play here.
   ◇ K x x x x   You would have overcalled 1 NT before;
   ♣ Q J x x x   or you would now pass and settle for a
                 small profit if you had a balanced hand
with heart strength. 2 NT here is played as "Unusual," and it asks
partner to take his *choice of the minor suits*.

Another common balancing situation is when an opening bid on
your *left* is passed around to you:

East	South	West	North
		1 ♡	Pass
Pass	?		

Suppose you, as South, hold:

7. ♠ Q 10 x x x   **How many high-card points can you ex-**
   ♡ x x   **pect partner to hold here?** Suppose we
   ◇ A x x   "give" opener 17, somewhat over mini-
   ♣ J x x   mum; and responder 3, about in the mid-
                  dle of his range. This still leaves partner
with an opening bid! You should balance with 1 ♠.

Note that you would *not* consider a 1 ♠ overcall if you were in
the *direct* seat. In choosing a balancing action in this situation, keep
in mind that *you expect partner to hold some strength*. ALL YOUR
ACTIONS, THEREFORE, ARE *SHADED*.

For instance, a 1 NT overcall in the balancing, or *passout,* seat
shows *less* than the same bid made in the direct position.

8. ♠ x x x   If a 1 ♡ opening is passed around to you,
   ♡ K J x   balance with 1 NT. This shows about
   ◇ A J x x 10-14 high-card points, and suggests
   ♣ Q x x   balanced pattern and a stopper in the op-
             ponent's suit.

Let's look at some other hands and decide what balancing action
you should choose.

East	South	West	North
		1 ♡	Pass
Pass	?		

9.   ♠ K x   Bid 2 ♣.
     ♡ x x
     ◊ A x x
     ♣ J x x x x x

10.   ♠ A Q J x x x   Bid *2 ♠*. *Jump* overcalls in the *direct* seat
     ♡ x x   are played as *mild preempts*. But it is silly
     ◊ A K x   to play a jump in the passout seat as pre-
     ♣ x x   emptive when the opponents have stopped
                         bidding. A *balancing* jump overcall is
intermediate, showing a good six or seven-card suit and about an
opening bid.

11.   ♠ A x x x   Double. You may *balance* with a takeout
     ♡ x   double with as little as 8 or 9 high-card
     ◊ K J x x   points if your distribution is ideal.
     ♣ J x x x

12.   ♠ A K x x   Double and plan to *raise* partner's re-
     ♡ x x   sponse, telling him that you have a sound
     ◊ K Q x x   hand for your takeout double and *weren't*
     ♣ K J x   just balancing with a weaker one.

13.   ♠ K Q x x x   Double, planning to bid your spades next.
     ♡ x x   You would not be strong enough to bid
     ◊ A Q x   this way in the direct seat and would have
     ♣ A x x   to overcall 1 ♠. But in the balancing posi-
                         tion, all your actions are *shaded*.

14.   ♠ A x   Double, planning to bid notrump at your
     ♡ K J x   next turn. Remember that a 1 NT overcall
     ◊ A K x x   in the balancing position shows 10-14
     ♣ Q J x x   HCP, so you must start with a double if
                         you have a strong balanced hand.

15.   ♠ x   Pass. The opponents may have a better
     ♡ A x x x   contract in spades, so don't give them a
     ◊ K x x x   chance to reach it.
     ♣ Q x x x

16. ♠ K Q x x x x   Reopen with a 2♡ *cuebid.* You suggest
    ♡ —   a huge offensive hand, invariably a one
    ◊ A   or two-suiter. Avoid starting with a take-
    ♣ K J x x x x   out double, since partner may pass for
                             penalties.

WHEN YOUR PARTNER BALANCES:

> WHEN PARTNER BALANCES, REMEMBER THAT HE
> COUNTED ON YOU FOR SUBSTANTIAL VALUES. YOU
> MUST *NOT* COMPETE FURTHER, TRY FOR GAME,
> DOUBLE IF THE OPPONENTS BID ON, OR TAKE ANY
> AGGRESSIVE ACTION UNLESS YOUR HAND CON-
> TAINS EXTRA HIGH CARDS OR UNUSUALLY GOOD
> DISTRIBUTION.

Let's look at some examples:

East	*South*	*West*	*North*
1♡	Pass	Pass	1♠
Pass	?		

1.   ♠ A J x   Pass. If partner had overcalled in the
     ♡ J x x   direct seat, you would have tried for
     ◊ K x x x   game. But he could have as little as 7 HCP
     ♣ A x x   for his balancing overcall.

East	*South*	*West*	*North*
1♡	Pass	Pass	Double
Pass	?		

2.   ♠ A J x x   Bid only 1♠. You would have jumped in
     ♡ A x x x   response to a direct takeout double, but
     ◊ Q x x   here partner could be very light. Remem-
     ♣ x x   ber, he *expects* you to have at least a fair
                       hand.

East	*South*	*West*	*North*
		1♡	Pass
2♡	Pass	Pass	2♠
Pass	Pass	3♡	Pass
Pass	?		

3.　♠ A Q x　　　　Pass. Partner bid your hand when he tried
　　♡ Q x x　　　　2 ♠. Be grateful that you now get to de-
　　◇ K x x x x　　fend 3 ♡ instead of 2 ♡. Partner's
　　♣ J x　　　　　balance has accomplished its purpose, so
　　　　　　　　　　you must not punish him by taking action.

WHEN *NOT* TO BALANCE:

We have already seen a couple of times when it may be wrong
to balance: when you have a strong holding in the opponents' suit;
when you fear they may find a *better* suit if you balance; when you
have values in their suit that will be wasted if your side declares the
hand.

Another situation is when the opponents stop low, *but the auction
suggests they do NOT have a fit.* In that case, the deal may be a misfit
all the way around, and any balancing action is very dangerous.

East	*South*	*West*	*North*
1 ◇	Pass	1 ♠	Pass
2 ◇	Pass	2 ♠	Pass
Pass	?		

As South, you hold:

♠ K x x　　　　　The opponents could have as many as 24
♡ K J 9 x x x　　HCP. They could have stopped bidding
◇ Q x x　　　　　in fear of a misfit. Furthermore, you have
♣ x　　　　　　　no reason to believe that your side has any
　　　　　　　　　fit. Opener could have six diamonds and
four hearts, responder could have six spades and three hearts, and
North could be void in hearts! The time to balance freely is when
the opponents have a good fit. Here a balancing action could get you
heavily penalized.

East	*South*	*West*	*North*
1 ◇	Pass	1 NT	Pass
Pass	??		

♠ x　　　　　　　Pass. West should have length in clubs
♡ A x x x　　　　since he failed to raise diamonds or bid
◇ Q x x　　　　　a major suit. Partner's length is in spades,
♣ K J 9 x x　　　since the opponents failed to find a fit in
　　　　　　　　　that suit.

Let's review the principle of balancing:

> WHEN THE OPPONENTS STOP BIDDING AT A LOW
> LEVEL, AND ESPECIALLY WHEN THEY HAVE A FIT,
> YOU SHOULD CONSIDER *BALANCING* WITH AN OVER-
> CALL OR A TAKEOUT DOUBLE. IF YOUR PARTNER
> BALANCES, REMEMBER THAT HE IS BIDDING YOUR
> CARDS. TAKE NO STRONG ACTION UNLESS YOU
> HAVE AN UNUSUAL HAND.

If the opponents' auction goes: 1♣ - 2♣ or 1◊ - 2◊, you will probably balance about 80% of the time; and you will often balance if they open and raise in a major suit and stop at the two level.

Another common situation is when an opening bid on your left is passed around to you. Let's list the possible balancing actions and compare them with the requirements for the same action in the *direct* position.

Action	Balancing (Passout) Seat	Direct Seat
Overcall	Less than an opening bid, as little as 7 HCP.	About an opening bid, maybe a little more.
Jump overcall	Good six or seven-card suit; about an opening bid in high cards.	Good suit, poor high-card strength.
1 NT	10-14 HCP, balanced pattern, usually a stopper in the opponent's suit.	16-18 HCP, balanced pattern, always a stopper in the opponent's suit.
Takeout Double	8-9 HCP or more.	Close to an opening bid in high cards or more.
Cuebid	A freakish one or two-suiter that will probably produce game.	A hand that would have opened with a forcing two-bid. Great defensive and playing strength.

Avoid balancing actions when your hand is weak; when you have such a strong holding in the opponent's suit that you are willing to defend (vulnerability is a consideration); when the opponents may be better off in some other suit; when the opponents have stopped low but the auction suggests they do *not* have a fit; or, in close cases, when you have values in the opponents' suit that will be useless if your side declares the hand.

TEST YOUR COMPREHENSION OF THE MATERIAL IN THIS CHAPTER:

QUIZ ON RECONSTRUCTING DECLARER'S HAND ON DEFENSE:

1.

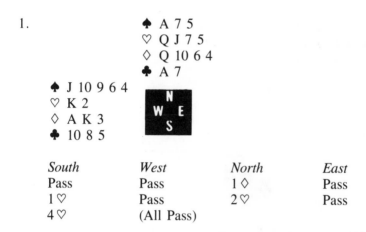

	♠ A 7 5
	♡ Q J 7 5
	◇ Q 10 6 4
	♣ A 7

♠ J 10 9 6 4
♡ K 2
◇ A K 3
♣ 10 8 5

South	West	North	East
Pass	Pass	1 ◇	Pass
1 ♡	Pass	2 ♡	Pass
4 ♡	(All Pass)		

You, West, lead the ♣ J. Declarer wins dummy's ace, dropping the queen from his hand. The ♡ Q is finessed to your king, and declarer ruffs your spade continuation. He draws another round of trumps, your partner playing the ten.

Next declarer plays the ♣ AKQ and ruffs a fourth round of clubs in dummy. East plays the jack on the last round. Declarer ruffs another spade in his hand and leads a diamond toward dummy. What is declarer's distribution? What do you play on the diamond lead?

141

2.

♠ Q 6
♥ K 7 5
⋄ Q 9 6 4
♣ A K J 4

♠ K 10 5
♥ Q 10 6 2
⋄ K 5
♣ 10 8 6 2

South	West	North	East
Pass	Pass	1 ♣	Pass
1 ⋄	Pass	2 ⋄	Pass
3 ⋄	Pass	5 ⋄	(All Pass)

You, West, lead the ♥2. Dummy plays low, partner plays the nine, and declarer wins the jack. Declarer leads the ⋄A and a low diamond. You win and partner's jack falls. What do you lead now?

3.

♠ 10 8 3
♥ Q 9 7
⋄ A Q J 10 4
♣ J 5

♠ K J 7 2
♥ A 5
⋄ 7 6
♣ Q 9 8 4 2

South opened 1 NT, North raised to 3 NT. You, West, lead the ♣4. Dummy wins the jack, declarer following with the ten. Declarer now leads a heart to his king, and you win the ace. What should you lead at this point?

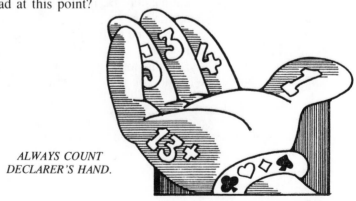

ALWAYS COUNT DECLARER'S HAND.

142

4.

	♠ Q 6
	♡ A 9 4
	◊ K J 6 4
	♣ Q J 6 5

♠ 8 7 4 3
♡ 5 3
◊ A 9 7 5
♣ K 9 2

```
        N
    W       E
        S
```

South	West	North	East
		1 ♣	Pass
1 ♠	Pass	1 NT	Pass
3 ♡	Pass	3 NT	Pass
4 ♡	(All Pass)		

You, West, lead the ◊ A, to which declarer follows low. What should you play at trick two?

SOLUTIONS:

1. Declarer has one spade, four clubs and no more than five hearts; so he had three diamonds at least. You should *duck* the diamond lead. If declarer lacks the ◊ J, he will probably play dummy's ten and lose three diamond tricks. Notice that you must do your counting *in advance* on this hand so that when declarer leads a diamond, you can duck *smoothly* with your ace and king. A long hesitation will tell declarer that you have strong diamonds.

2. Lead a spade. Declarer failed to open the bidding and is known to have the ◊ A and the ♡ A and ♡ J. So partner must have the ♠ A.

3. Declarer is known to have the ♣ AK and the ♡ K, and he surely has the ◊ K too. If he needed to finesse in diamonds to set up the suit, he would do that *first*. So we know about *13* of declarer's high-card points. His spades, therefore cannot be as good as ace-queen. That would give him 19 points, too many for his 1 NT opening.

   A spade shift must be safe, since partner must have one of the missing honors, and it is really the only chance for the defense. Declarer had five diamond tricks and three club tricks to begin with, and the ♡ Q is now a winner. The contract will be made unless the defenders can cash the setting tricks in spades.

4.　Lead a club. The bidding indicates that declarer has at least ten cards in hearts and spades; therefore, three or fewer cards in the minor suits. Even if you lead a club and find declarer with A-x, you lose nothing. He would discard his club loser on the ◇ K anyway. But if *partner* has the ♣ A, the defenders need to cash their club tricks right away, before declarer throws one of his club losers away on the ◇ K.

QUIZ ON BALANCING:

I.　Your right-hand opponent opened 1 ♡ , left-hand opponent raised to 2 ♡ , passed around to you. How many high-card points would you expect partner to hold if your hand were:

(a)　♠ K x x　　　　(b)　♠ A J x x
　　　♡ x x x　　　　　　　♡ J x
　　　◇ K x x x　　　　　　◇ A x x x
　　　♣ J x x　　　　　　　♣ Q x x

II.　Your right-hand opponent opened 1 ♠ , left-hand opponent raised to 2 ♠ , passed around to you. What action do you take with these hands:

(a)　♠ x x　　　　　(b)　♠ J x x
　　　♡ A x x x　　　　　　♡ K x x
　　　◇ K x x x　　　　　　◇ A x x x
　　　♣ Q x x　　　　　　　♣ K x x

(c)　♠ K J x　　　　(d)　♠ A x x
　　　♡ Q x x　　　　　　　♡ Q x x x
　　　◇ A x x x　　　　　　◇ A Q x x
　　　♣ Q x x　　　　　　　♣ J x

(e)　♠ Q J 10 x　　　(f)　♠ x x x
　　　♡ K x x x　　　　　　♡ K Q 10 x x
　　　◇ A x x　　　　　　　◇ A J 10
　　　♣ J x　　　　　　　　♣ x x

(g)　♠ J x x　　　　(h)　♠ x x x x
　　　♡ x　　　　　　　　　♡ x x
　　　◇ Q J x x x x　　　　◇ J x
　　　♣ K J x　　　　　　　♣ A K x x x

III. Your left-hand opponent opened 1 ◇ , passed around to you. What action do you take with these hands:

(a) ♠ A J x
    ♡ K x x x x
    ◇ x x
    ♣ x x x

(b) ♠ A x x
    ♡ Q x
    ◇ x x x
    ♣ K J x x x

(c) ♠ K J x x
    ♡ Q x x
    ◇ x x
    ♣ K x x x

(d) ♠ A K x x x
    ♡ A x x
    ◇ x x
    ♣ A J x

(e) ♠ x x x
    ♡ A Q x
    ◇ A Q x
    ♣ K J x x

(f) ♠ K J x
    ♡ A x x
    ◇ x x x
    ♣ J x x x

(g) ♠ A x
    ♡ K Q J x x x
    ◇ A x x
    ♣ x x

(h) ♠ x x x
    ♡ Q x x
    ◇ A J x
    ♣ K J x x

(i) ♠ A K x x
    ♡ A Q x x
    ◇ x x
    ♣ K x x

(j) ♠ K Q x x x
    ♡ A Q x x x x
    ◇ —
    ♣ Q x

(k) ♠ x x x
    ♡ A x x
    ◇ J x
    ♣ J x x x x

(l) ♠ x
    ♡ J x x x
    ◇ A J 10 x
    ♣ Q x x x

IV. The bidding has proceeded:

East	South	West	North
		1 ♡	Pass
2 ♡	Pass	Pass	2 ♠
Pass	Pass	3 ♡	Pass
Pass	?		

As South, with neither side vulnerable, what action do you take with these hands:

(a) ♠ A x x
    ♡ Q J 9 x
    ◊ Q x x
    ♣ x x x

(b) ♠ A Q x
    ♡ J x x
    ◊ K x x x x
    ♣ Q x

(c) ♠ A J x x
    ♡ x
    ◊ A x x x
    ♣ J x x x

V. Which of the following auctions by the opponents suggest that you balance?

(a) 1 ♡ - 1 ♠
    2 ♡ - Pass

(b) 1 ♡ - 1 NT
    Pass

(c) 1 ◊ - 2 ◊
    Pass

(d) 1 ♡ - 1 ♠
    2 ♠ - Pass

(e) 1 ♣ - 1 ♡
    2 ♣ - 2 ♡
    Pass

(f) 1 NT - Pass

(g) 1 ♡ - 1 NT
    2 ♣ - 2 ♡
    Pass

(h) 1 ◊   - 1 ♠
    1 NT - Pass

(i) 1 ♡ - 1 ♠
    2 ♣ - Pass

VI. What action do you take in these situations as South?

(a)

East	South	West	North
1 ♡	Pass	1 NT	Pass
Pass	??		

♠ K x
♡ A x x x
◇ K 10 x x
♣ A x x

(b)

East	South	West	North
		3 ♡	Pass
Pass	??		

♠ K Q x x
♡ x
◇ A x x x
♣ K x x x

(c)

East	South	West	North
1 ◇	Pass	1 NT	Pass
Pass	??		

♠ x x
♡ K x x
◇ J x x
♣ A Q x x x

(d)

East	South	West	North
		1 ♣	Pass
2 ♣	Pass	3 ♣	Pass
Pass	??		

♠ A J x x
♡ K J x x x
◇ x
♣ x x x

(e)

East	South	West	North
		Pass	Pass
1 ♡	Pass	1 ♠	Pass
Pass	??		

(e) ♠ x x x
♡ K 10 x
◇ K Q J x
♣ Q 10 x

(f)

East	South	West	North
		1 ◇	Pass
1 ♠	Pass	2 ♠	Pass
Pass	??		

(f) ♠ x x
♡ K J x x
◇ A x x
♣ J x x x

SOLUTIONS:

I. (a) 10-14 HCP.
    (b) 5-9 HCP.
II. (a) Double.
    (b) Pass. Too risky to balance.
    (c) Pass.
    (d) Double.
    (e) Pass.
    (f) 3 ♡.
    (g) 3 ◇.
    (h) 3 ♣.
III. (a) 1 ♡.
    (b) 2 ♣ or 1 NT.
    (c) Double.
    (d) Double first, then bid spades.
    (e) Double, then bid notrump.
    (f) Double (a minimum).
    (g) 2 ♡.
    (h) 1 NT.
    (i) Double and bid further.
    (j) 2 ◇.

	(k)	Pass.
	(l)	Pass.
IV.	(a)	Pass.
	(b)	Pass.
	(c)	3♠. You have more than partner can reasonably expect.
V.	(a)	Perhaps with a very suitable hand.
	(b)	No.
	(c)	Yes.
	(d)	Yes.
	(e)	No.
	(f)	No.
	(g)	No. If responder had true heart support, he would have raised to begin with.
	(h)	No.
	(i)	No.
VI.	(a)	Pass. If your heart intermediates were better, you might risk a double, which partner might be able to pass for penalties.
	(b)	Double. You would need more to double in the direct seat, but this is enough in the balancing position.
	(c)	Pass. West must have clubs since he did not raise diamonds or bid a major suit.
	(d)	Double. Partner should have a few points and shortness in clubs, therefore length in at least one of the majors.
	(e)	1 NT. Don't worry about the spades. Partner is likely to have a stopper, and even if he does not, you will not be hurt badly at the one level.
	(f)	Double. Takeout for the unbid suits. This auction suggests you balance.

Chapter 9

STRONG AND WEAK TWO-BIDS
PREEMPTIVE OPENINGS

STRONG AND WEAK TWO-BIDS
PREEMPTIVE OPENINGS

I.   Opening bids of *TWO OF A SUIT* have traditionally shown hands
     with which opener expects to make game *no matter what* his
     partner has. If you hold, as dealer:

> ♠ A K x
> ♡ A K Q 10 x x
> ◇ A J 10
> ♣ x

you can't open *1♡*, since partner would pass with:

> ♠ x x
> ♡ x x x
> ◇ Q x x x
> ♣ x x x x

and your side would miss an easy game. While an opening *4♡* bid
would get you to game, it would leave no room to investigate slam.
(As you probably know, a 4♡ opening shows a different kind of
hand.)

   In deciding whether to open with a STRONG TWO-BID, it is easier
NOT to think in terms of *points*. Altough many texts give point-count
requirements for this action (25 points with a five-card suit, etc.),
the actual requirements are:

1.   Enough *PLAYING TRICKS* to make game.
2.   At least 4 *QUICK TRICKS*.

1. *PLAYING TRICKS. Decide how many tricks you will take even if the dummy puts down the worst hand your imagination can devise. Consider the hand above. This hand should produce six heart tricks, two spades, one diamond, and maybe another diamond if a diamond is led or if partner has so much as the queen or length. So the PLAYING-TRICK requirement is met. Let's look at some other hands:*

♠ A K J 10 x
♡ K Q J 9 x
◇ A K
♣ x

How many playing tricks? Four or five in spades, probably four in hearts, two in diamonds. You have the PLAYING TRICKS for a strong two-bid.

♠ A
♡ A K J x
◇ A Q x x
♣ A x x x

A lot of points, but not many playing tricks. You must risk an opening bid of just one. You *cannot guarantee a game* if partner has a balanced pile of nothing.

2. *QUICK TRICKS. A STRONG TWO-BID promises cards that will take tricks no matter what happens in the bidding, and the ability to penalize the opponents if they bid. If you hold:*

♠ A K Q J x x x x
♡ —
◇ Q J 10 x
♣ x

you can expect to take ten tricks at a spade contract but you should not open with a strong two-bid — your *defensive* strength is poor. If the opponents, who may have substantial high-card strength and distribution, start bidding, they may make what they bid. Hands like this may be opened *1 ♠* or *4 ♠* (as we will see), but *not 2 ♠*. QUICK TRICKS, as you know, are the measure of a hand's *defensive* worth and are counted according to the following table:

A	1	QT
AK in same suit	2	QTs
AQ in same suit	.............................1½	QTs
KQ in same suit	1	QT
K	.... ½	QT

A STRONG TWO-BID REQUIRES AT LEAST 4 QUICK TRICKS.

RESPONDING TO A STRONG TWO-BID:

Since opener has stated that game is certain, RESPONDER MUST NOT PASS. Often he will respond 2 NT, which shows weakness and warns opener not to expect much in dummy. A direct jump to game in opener's suit is also a weakish response. It shows *excellent support* but *denies* any side first or second-round control. Any other response, such as a single raise or a bid of a new suit, is *positive*. Responder says he would have responded had the opening bid been *one* of a suit, and *slam* is a possibility.

Let's look at a few hands and see what responder would do over an opening bid of 2♡.

1. ♠ J x x x   Respond 2 NT. Remember, you must bid.
    ♡ x x x   Furthermore, if partner rebids 3♡ over
    ◊ x x   your 2 NT, *you must raise to 4♡*. After
    ♣ x x x x   partner opens 2♡, the auction must not
    die until game is reached (unless you decide to double the opponents). (Note of interest: *some partnerships* play that responder *may pass* if opener simply rebids his suit after a negative response. Such pairs require less in playing tricks to open with a strong two-bid.)

2. ♠ Q 10 x x x x Respond 2 NT to show your weak hand.
    ♡ x x   A 2♠ response would be positive,
    ◊ x x x   suggesting more strength.
    ♣ J x

3. ♠ K Q x x   This is a *minimum 2♠* response.
    ♡ x x
    ◊ Q x x
    ♣ x x x

152

4. ♠ x x
   ♡ K x
   ◇ A Q J x x
   ♣ J x x x

Respond 3 ◇. You will probably wind up in a slam. Nevertheless, notice that you *do not need to jump* at this stage.

5. ♠ x x
   ♡ Q x x
   ◇ J x x x
   ♣ A x x x

Respond 3 ♡.

6. ♠ A x
   ♡ K J x
   ◇ K x x x
   ♣ x x x x

You may have a grand slam, but respond only 3 ♡ to begin with, to set the trump suit.

7. ♠ x x
   ♡ Q J x x x
   ◇ x x x
   ♣ x x x

Respond *4♡*. Good support, bad hand.

II.   The trouble with STRONG TWO-BIDS is that they don't occur often enough to satisfy players who like to bid. Many partnerships agree that *their* opening two-bids will show a *different* kind of hand. They play *WEAK* TWO-BIDS. What kind of two-bids *you* play is up to you and your favorite partner. But WEAK two-bids have acquired a large following.

A WEAK TWO-BID is an action that is *both preemptive* and *descriptive*. The requirements are:

---

1.   A GOOD SIX-CARD SUIT.
2.   From 6 to 12 HIGH-CARD POINTS. Typically, most of your high cards will be *in the suit you bid*.
3.   At least 1 but no more than 2 QUICK TRICKS.

A good WEAK TWO-BID should be oriented for play only in your own suit. You should *not,* for example, open 2 ♠ with a hand that would make a good *dummy* for a contract in clubs or hearts. *Avoid* opening a weak two-bid with a *side void* — your partner cannot judge how many tricks the combined hands will produce.

What if you are playing WEAK TWO-BIDS and you are dealt a game-going hand? You open *2♣*. WEAK TWO-BIDS are played in *spades, hearts* and *diamonds only*. Opener bids *2♣* with *all* his

153

very strong hands, regardless of what suit he holds. His *later* bidding will clarify *what kind of strong hand* he has.

Let's look at a few possible WEAK TWO-BIDS. You are the dealer, with neither side vulnerable:

1. ♠ K Q J x x x   Open 2♠. This is a classic hand for a
   ♡ x   WEAK TWO-BID.
   ◊ K x x
   ♣ x x x

2. ♠ Q 10 x x x x   Pass. Your suit is too poor to open 2♠.
   ♡ K Q x   Too many of your values are elsewhere.
   ◊ K x
   ♣ x x

3. ♠ K Q J x x x   Open *1♠*. This hand is too good for a
   ♡ A x   weak two-bid.
   ◊ Q x
   ♣ x x x

4. ♠ Q J 10 x x x   Open 2♠, although you would prefer that
   ♡ x x   the ◊ A were the ♠*A*.
   ◊ A Q x
   ♣ x x

5. ♠ A 10 x x x x   Pass. A 2♠ opening would make it hard
   ♡ K x x   to get to a good heart or club contract.
   ◊ x
   ♣ Q J x

6. ♠ K Q 10 x x x   Pass. Avoid opening a weak two-bid with
   ♡ —   a side-suit *void*.
   ◊ A x x
   ♣ x x x x

7. ♠ A Q J 10 x x   Open 2♠.
   ♡ x x
   ◊ Q x x x
   ♣ x

8. ♠ A K x x x x   Open *1♠*. You have *too many Quick*
    ♡ A x   *Tricks* to open with a weak two-bid.
    ◊ x x x
    ♣ x

RESPONDING TO A WEAK TWO-BID:

There are several options:

---

1. A NEW SUIT is forcing. It asks opener to show support,
    rebid his suit if it is especially strong, or bid another suit
    in which he has a high card.
2. 2 NT is forcing and, as most partnerships play, asks opener
    to show an *ace or king* he holds in *some other suit*. If
    unable to do that, opener may *rebid* his own suit *cheaply*
    or *raise to 3 NT* if he has a solid suit that will run at
    notrump.
3. A SINGLE RAISE is played as an additional preempt.
    Responder is *not* interested in game and opener should
    not bid further.
4. A RAISE TO GAME may be bid with the expectation of
    making, or it may be purely preemptive. One advantage
    of the WEAK TWO-BID is that responder can often tell
    immediately how much both sides can probably make. He
    can bid game confidently or take further preemptive action.

Your partner opened 2 ♡ as dealer, with neither side vulnerable,
and your right-hand opponent passed.

1. ♠ K J x x   Pass. Your best hope is that the opponents
    ♡ x   will bid.
    ◊ A x x x
    ♣ A J x x

2. ♠ x x   Bid 3 ♡. You won't make this, but the
    ♡ Q x   opponents could be cold for game in
    ◊ A x x x x   spades and you will make it hard for them
    ♣ Q x x x   to bid.

3. ♠ A J x   3 NT. Bid what you think you can make.
    ♡ K x x
    ◊ Q J x x
    ♣ A Q x

4. ♠ A K x
   ♡ A x
   ◇ A J x x x x
   ♣ J x

Bid 2 NT, (forcing). If partner bids 3 ♣, showing the ♣A or ♣K, you can try 3 NT. If he has nothing in clubs, you must bid 4 ♡.·

5. ♠ K Q 10 x x x
   ♡ x
   ◇ A K Q
   ♣ Q x x

Bid 2 ♠, hoping partner has support and will show it. If he does, you can bid game in spades. A response in a new suit is *forcing.*

6. ♠ A K x x
   ♡ x x
   ◇ A K J x x
   ♣ K x

Bid 4 ♡ (but no more).

7. ♠ x x
   ♡ Q x x x
   ◇ K Q x x x
   ♣ J x

Bid 4 ♡. The opponents must be cold for 4 ♠, so make it as hard as possible for them to get there. This bid is strictly *pre-emptive.*

OPENING 2 ♣:

If you play WEAK TWO-BIDS, *all* your *strong* hands are opened *2 ♣*. The requirements for a 2 ♣ opening are the same as for *any* strong two-bid: sure playing tricks and good defensive strength.

There are slight changes in the *responses* to 2 ♣. The *negative response is 2 ◇, not 2 NT.* The advantages of this scheme (if opener has a *strong major suit,* he can now show his suit at the *two* level and save bidding space) outweigh the drawbacks (if responder has a good hand with a *diamond* suit, he must bid *3 ◇* to show a positive response). *A response of 2 NT to 2 ♣* is *positive,* showing a balanced hand with at least 7 high-card points.

If you play WEAK TWO-BIDS, notice that there are now *two* ways to "open 2 NT." You can open 2 NT, or you can open 2 ♣ and bid 2 NT *next.* We can improve our bidding system by taking advantage of this:

Using *STRONG* TWO-BIDS:

Open one of a suit and jump in notrump next:	19-21 high-card points
Open 2 NT:	22-24
Open 3 NT:	25-27

Using *WEAK* TWO-BIDS:

Open one of a suit and jump in notrump next:	19-20
Open 2 NT:	21-22
Open 2 ♣, rebid 2 NT:	23-24
Open 2 ♣, rebid 3 NT:	25-26
Open 3 NT:	27-28

Using *weak* two-bids, each bid shows a *more narrowly-defined hand,* which makes the bidding *more accurate.*

III. While opening bids of *two* may be *strong,* opening bids of *three or more* are *weak* and *preemptive,* Opener's purpose is *not* to discover what *his* side can make, but to *use up space* in the auction so that the *opponents* can no longer exchange information and find *their* best contract. The time to make a preemptive bid is:

1.	When your hand offers little hope in *defense* of an opposing game or slam. And . . .
2.	When you hold a long, strong suit that you can rely on for tricks.

Suppose you are dealer with:

♠ K Q J x x x x
♡ x
♢ J 10 x
♣ x x

You should be anxious for spades to be trumps since your hand may not take a single trick otherwise. Since the opponents may bid and make a game or slam if you give them a good chance, open *3 ♠.*

Note that when you *preempt,* you do not expect to make what you bid. In fact, if you open 3 ♠ on our example hand, and partner puts down:

♠ x x x
♡ x x x
◇ x x x
♣ x x x x

you will go down three tricks, and you will certainly be doubled. However, if partner's hand is worthless, the opponents can make a grand slam in any strain (except spades). You would show a tremendous profit by allowing them to score 500 points against 3 ♠ doubled, as opposed to what they could reap if you let them bid carefully to their grand slam.

There is, of course, no law against your partner having a *good* hand. If he has a few tricks, you will make your 3 ♠ bid. Perhaps he will even raise you to 4 ♠. But the purpose of your 3 ♠ bid is to keep the opponents from bidding accurately if *they* have the balance of power.

Note that, to preempt, you need an *excellent suit.* If you do not have a sure source of tricks, the penalty may be too high. You prefer a suit that *will produce six or seven tricks* (depending on the *vulnerability*).

Let's look at some hands and decide what your action would be as dealer, with neither side vulnerable.

1. ♠ x   Open 3 ♡.
   ♡ K Q 10 x x x x
   ◇ x x
   ♣ Q 10 x

2. ♠ Q x x x x x x   Pass. A preempt could be too expensive.
   ♡ x x x
   ◇ x
   ♣ x x

3. ♠ A x   Open *1 ♡.* You won't always preempt just
   ♡ K Q J x x x x   because you have a seven-card suit. This
   ◇ Q x   is a normal opening of *one.*
   ♣ J x

4. ♠ Q x   Pass. You have bits and pieces that are
♡ K J 10 x x x x   potential tricks on defense, and you have
◊ J x x   your normal share of the high cards.
♣ K   There is no reason to panic and assume
the opponents are about to bid a game and
make it.

5. ♠ x   Pass or *1* ♡. Avoid a preempt with a solid
♡ A K Q x x x x   suit. You might have a couple of *defensive*
◊ x x   tricks.
♣ J x x

After a preemptive opening, responder is "captain." Suppose you start with 3 ♠ on:

♠ K Q J x x x x
♡ —
◊ J x x
♣ x x x

Your left-hand opponent overcalls 4 ♡ and your partner doubles. *You must pass.* You told partner what kind of hand you had when you preempted. Respect his judgment.

The *most* important factor that influences your preemptive strategy is the *vulnerability*. The *best* time to preempt is when the *opponents are vulnerable* and *your side is not.* They will be anxious to clinch the rubber and reluctant to settle for a small penalty by doubling you, so your preempt may goad them into bidding. They will find that accuracy is more difficult. The *worst* time to preempt is when *you are vulnerable* and *they are not.* They will be more inclined to double you, so you must be able to come close to making your bid.

RESPONDING TO PREEMPTS:

To raise partner's preempt *you need Quick Tricks,* not just points. Queens and jacks in the side suits are of doubtful value to partner, who may have singletons and doubletons in those suits. If partner opens 3 ♠ at equal vulnerability, however, you may count on him for about *six or seven winners,* so if your hand contains three or four Quick Tricks, you can raise him to game.

159

Suppose that opener bids 3♡, with no one vulnerable.

1. ♠ A K x x   Bid 4♡
    ♡ A x
    ◇ A J 10 x
    ♣ x x x

2. ♠ K Q x   Pass.
    ♡ J x
    ◇ Q J x x
    ♣ K Q x x

3. ♠ A K x x   Bid 4♡. You do not need support for
    ♡ x   hearts when partner's suit is self-sustain-
    ◇ A x x x   ing. *Do not consider bidding 3 NT.* You
    ♣ A Q x x   can't expect to establish and cash partner's
                           suit since his hand will lack entries.

4. ♠ x x   Bid 4♡. You will go down a couple, but
    ♡ K x x   the opponents can surely make 4♠; so
    ◇ A J x x   you tack on a little preempt of your own.
    ♣ x x x x

5. ♠ K J x   Bid 3 NT. Notice that you have a "fit"
    ♡ A x x   for hearts and expect to run partner's suit.
    ◇ K Q 10
    ♣ Q J x x

6. ♠ A K J x x x   Bid 3♠. A response in a new suit is *forc-*
    ♡ x   *ing.* This will help you to look for a game
    ◇ A K x x   or slam in another suit.
    ♣ A x

PREEMPTS OF MORE THAN THREE:

An opening three bid is usually based on a good *seven*-card suit. If you are dealt an even longer suit, it may be safe (and desirable) for you to open at the four or five level. Say that you are dealer with neither side vulnerable:

1. ♠ K Q J x x x x x   Open 4 ♠. With an extra winner in your
    ♡ —   suit, you can afford to preempt a little
    ◊ x x   higher.
    ♣ Q x x

2. ♠ —   Open 5 ♣!
    ♡ x
    ◊ Q 10 x
    ♣ K Q 10 x x x x x x

TEST YOUR COMPREHENSION OF THE MATERIAL IN THIS CHAPTER:

QUIZ ON STRONG TWO-BIDS:

I. Playing strong two-bids, what do you call as dealer with:

1. ♠ A Q J 10 x x   2. ♠ K J x x x
    ♡ A K Q x   ♡ K J x x x
    ◊ A x   ◊ A K
    ♣ x   ♣ A

3. ♠ A Q x   4. ♠ A K J 10 x
    ♡ A J x   ♡ A x
    ◊ A J x x x   ◊ A K Q x x
    ♣ A K   ♣ Q

5. ♠ A x
    ♡ A K x
    ◊ x
    ♣ A K J x x x x

II. Partner opens 2 ♡ (strong). What do you respond with:

1. ♠ Q J x x x x   2. ♠ A Q x x
    ♡ x x   ♡ K x x
    ◊ x x x   ◊ x x
    ♣ x x   ♣ x x x x

3. ♠ x x   4. ♠ x x
    ♡ J x x x   ♡ K Q x x
    ◊ x x x   ◊ x x x
    ♣ x x x x   ♣ x x x x

5. ♠ x x x
    ♡ x
    ◊ A x x x
    ♣ A J x x x

QUIZ ON WEAK TWO-BIDS:

III. Playing weak two-bids, what do you call as dealer with:

1. ♠ J 10 x x x x   2. ♠ x
    ♡ A x   ♡ K Q 10 x x x
    ◊ K x x   ◊ K J x
    ♣ x x   ♣ x x x

3. ♠ A Q J x x x   4. ♠ A x x x x x
    ♡ x   ♡ K x x
    ◊ Q J x   ◊ x
    ♣ x x x   ♣ Q J x

5. ♠ A 10 x x x x
    ♡ K x
    ◊ A x x
    ♣ x x

IV. Partner opens 2 ♡ (weak). What do you respond with:

1. ♠ A J x x   2. ♠ A K x x
    ♡ x x   ♡ J x
    ◊ A J x x   ◊ A K J x
    ♣ Q J x   ♣ x x x

3. ♠ K J x x   4. ♠ x x
    ♡ K x   ♡ A x
    ◊ A K Q x   ◊ A x x x x
    ♣ x x x   ♣ J x x x

5. ♠ x
    ♡ K J x x
    ◊ K J x x x
    ♣ J x x

V. Playing weak two-bids, what do you call as dealer with:

1. ♠ A K Q 10 x x   2. ♠ A K x
    ♡ A x   ♡ K x x
    ◊ A K x x   ◊ A Q x x
    ♣ x   ♣ A K x

3. ♠ A J x x   4. ♠ x
    ♡ x   ♡ K x x
    ◊ A K Q x   ◊ x x x
    ♣ A Q x x   ♣ K Q J x x x

5. ♠ A x
    ♡ A K x
    ◊ A K J x x x x
    ♣ x

VI. Playing weak two-bids, partner opens 2♣. What do you respond with:

1. ♠ x x x   2. ♠ x x
    ♡ x x x   ♡ A x x
    ◊ x x x   ◊ K Q x x x
    ♣ x x x x   ♣ x x x

3. ♠ Q x x   4. ♠ Q J x x x x
    ♡ K x x   ♡ x x
    ◊ Q J x   ◊ x x x
    ♣ J x x x   ♣ J x

5. ♠ A Q J x x
    ♡ x x
    ◊ x x
    ♣ J x x x

QUIZ ON PREEMPTIVE OPENINGS:

VII. With neither side vulnerable, what do you call as dealer with:

1. ♠ K Q J x x x x
   ♡ x x
   ◊ J x x
   ♣ x

2. ♠ x
   ♡ Q J 10 x x x x
   ◊ Q J x
   ♣ x x

3. ♠ A 10 x x x x x
   ♡ J x
   ◊ K x
   ♣ Q x

4. ♠ A Q J x x x x
   ♡ Q x
   ◊ K x x
   ♣ x

5. ♠ K Q J x x x x x
   ♡ —
   ◊ Q x x
   ♣ x x

VIII. With neither side vulnerable, partner opens 3♠ as dealer. How do you respond with:

1. ♠ x
   ♡ A K x x
   ◊ A x x x
   ♣ A J x x

2. ♠ A x x
   ♡ Q J x
   ◊ Q J x
   ♣ A Q x x

3. ♠ J x x
   ♡ x
   ◊ A x x x
   ♣ x x x x x

4. ♠ K x
   ♡ Q x x
   ◊ K Q x x
   ♣ K J x x

5. ♠ K x x
   ♡ x
   ◊ A K Q x x
   ♣ A J x x

164

SOLUTIONS:

I.   1.   2♠
    2.   1♠
    3.   2 NT
    4.   2♠
    5.   2♣

II.   1.   2 NT
    2.   3♡
    3.   2 NT
    4.   4♡
    5.   3♣

III.   1.   Pass
    2.   2♡
    3.   2♠
    4.   Pass
    5.   Pass or 1♠

IV.   1.   Pass
    2.   4♡
    3.   2 NT, intending to bid 3 NT if partner has a high card in clubs.
    4.   3♡, an additional preempt to keep the opponents out of spades.
    5.   4♡, preemptive. The opponents can make at least 4♠

V.   1.   2♣
    2.   2♣, intending to rebid 2 NT.
    3.   1♣, not enough *tricks* to open 2♣.
    4.   Pass
    5.   2♣

VI.   1.   2♢
    2.   3♢
    3.   2 NT
    4.   2♢
    5.   2♠

VII.   1.   3♠
       2.   3♡
       3.   Pass. Too much potential defense to preempt.
       4.   1♠
       5.   4♠

VIII. 1.   4♠, to make.
       2.   3NT
       3.   4♠, preemptive
       4.   Pass
       5.   4 NT, Blackwood

TRY TO RELAX WHEN YOU'RE DUMMY.

Chapter 10

THINKING:
CARD COMBINATIONS AS DECLARER
LOOSE ENDS IN THE BIDDING

THINKING: CARD COMBINATIONS AS DECLARER

Let's start with a problem in declarer play:

♠ A Q x
♡ K x x'x x
◊ Q x x
♣ Q 10

♠ K J x
♡ A x
◊ K J x
♣ A K x x x

You have reached 6 NT, and the opening lead is a diamond. The ace wins on your right and a diamond is returned. To make this contract, you need five tricks from clubs. **Should you lead a club to dummy's ten or play off your high clubs, hoping for an even split?**

A 3-3 club break is less than an even chance, about 36% in fact. A finesse of the ♣10, on the other hand, will produce five tricks whenever the jack is on your left, provided the suit splits no worse than 4-2. The odds are only a little less than the 50-50 chance of the winning finesse. So the finesse of the ♣10 is best.

Throughout this book, we have talked about establishing tricks. In this chapter, we will look at how certain common combinations of cards are handled to best advantage.

1. As seen above, you may need to know the *best percentage play* to win the *maximum* number of tricks in a suit.
2. With certain card combinations, *correct play will assure* the maximum number of tricks.

For instance, with:

A 10 x x   opposite   K Q 9 x x

play the king or queen first. You take five tricks even if either opponent has all the missing cards. If you carelessly cash the ace first,
you lose a trick if you find:

$$A\ 10\ x\ x$$
$$J\ x\ x\ x$$
$$K\ Q\ 9\ x\ x$$

The techniques involved here have been called "security" plays.

3.   You may need to *insure* only a certain number of tricks.
A "safety" play is like an insurance policy. You may *give
up* the best play for *the maximum* number of tricks but
you *guard against a loss* of tricks you cannot afford. Look
at this example:

$$A\ Q\ x\ x\ x$$

$$x\ x\ x\ x$$

If you need *five* tricks from this suit, you must finesse the queen,
hoping for the doubleton king onside. But suppose you need only
four tricks. Let's say this is your trump suit in a small slam, and
you have no losers outside of trumps. **What should you do?** You
should *cash the trump ace before leading toward the queen.* You make
your four tricks whenever possible (if your right-hand opponent has
K-J-x or K-10-x, you can't avoid defeat), and you avoid the embar-
rassment of losing a first-round finesse to the *singleton* king and losing another trick later.

Obviously, you must *count your tricks* so you will know whether
to play safe or for the maximum.

In each example below, assume that the bidding and play have provided no information to influence how you attack the suit. *Entries* are plentiful, unless otherwise stated.

1. A J 10

    x x x

    TWO tricks. Lead low to the jack. If that loses, lead low to the ten next.

2. A J 10 x x

    x x x x

    FOUR tricks. It is better to double-finesse. Playing the ace first is almost as good.

3. A J 10 x x x

    x x x x

    FIVE tricks. Lead low to the jack (if left-hand opponents plays low). This is a "security" play which guards against K-Q-x on your left.

4. A K J 10 x

    x x x

    FIVE tricks. Cash the ace or king, in case right-hand opponent has the singleton queen. Then lead low to the jack.

5. A K J x x

    x x x x

    FIVE tricks. This is the old "eight-ever, nine-never" position. It is fractionally better to play off the ace and king.

6. A Q 10

    x x x

    THREE tricks. Lead low to the ten, hoping that both the king and jack are onside.

7. A Q 9 x x

    J x x x x

    FIVE tricks. It is best to *finesse* for a missing king with up to ten cards in your suit. Be careful to *lead the jack* in case your left-hand opponent holds K-10-x.

8. A K J 10 x x

    x x

    SIX tricks. Take a first round finesse to the jack or ten. You lose to the singleton queen offside, but you gain if right-hand opponent has a small singleton, which is *four times more likely*.

9. A x x x

    Q 10 9 8

    THREE tricks. Lead the queen and duck if it isn't covered. If it loses to the king, lead the eight next and duck it.

10. A x x x   THREE tricks. Play the ace and lead low toward your hand. If right-hand opponent

    Q 10 x x   plays low, your percentage play is the ten, winning if right-hand opponent has K-J-x-x. You cannot double-finesse as in the last example, since you lack good intermediates.

11. A x x   FOUR tricks. Play the ace and low to the jack. You must hope for right-hand op-

    K J x x   ponent to hold Q-x-x. For THREE tricks, the "safety" play is to cash the king and ace, and only then lead toward the jack. You'll avoid losing a finesse to the doubleton queen and losing another trick later.

12. A 10 x   TWO tricks. Lead low to the queen. If that loses, lead low to the ten.

    Q x x

13. A 10 x x   FOUR tricks. Play the ace and lead low toward the queen. This is your best shot

    Q 9 x x x   with *nine* cards in your suit.

14. A 10 x x   FIVE tricks. Lead low toward dummy and put in the ten if left-hand opponent

    Q 9 x x x x   plays low. This is a "safety" play which guards against K-J-x on your left. (If left-hand opponent is void, win the ace, lead to your queen.)

15. A J 9   TWO tricks. Lead low to the nine. If that loses to the king or queen, lead low to the

    x x x   jack next. You hope that left-hand opponent has the ten plus one other honor.

"LOOSE ENDS" IN THE BIDDING

We have surveyed the entire structure of "Standard American" bidding in this book. Now we will mention minor points of interest.

I. LIGHT OPENINGS

Many players are in the habit of opening the bidding on sub-minimum values in third position, in order to direct a lead and get

in a mild preempt in anticipation of the opponents' bidding. Light openings can be effective, *provided certain conditions are met.*

1. You must still have the minimum *two defensive tricks* that a normal opening suggests. Doubling the opponents will be impossible if your partner cannot trust your opening bid to produce some defensive tricks.

    ♠ J x
    ♡ Q J x x x
    ◊ A x x
    ♣ Q J x

Pass this hand in third seat. Your defensive values are lacking.

2. You must be able to *pass any response* partner makes. If you rebid, you suggest a legitimate, sound opening.

    ♠ x
    ♡ A 10 x x x
    ◊ K Q x
    ♣ Q x x x

Pass this hand in third seat. Partner is likely to respond 1 ♠, and you would be stuck. You couldn't bid again, having opened light; but partner will not like your spade "support" if you have to table this hand as dummy for a spade contract.

3. The lead of your suit should be desirable against an opposing contract.

    ♠ A x
    ♡ A x x
    ◊ J x x x x
    ♣ Q x x

Pass this hand in third seat. You do not want to suggest a diamond lead.

Here are some hands to open after two passes:

♠ A K x x x	♠ x x	♠ x x x
♡ J x	♡ A Q 10 x x	♡ A x x
◇ K x x	◇ J x x	◇ K Q J x x
♣ x x x	♣ A x x	♣ J x
1 ♣	1 ♡	1 ◇

Notice that, in each hand, the requirements listed above are present.

On some occasions, the fact that you plan to pass partner's response affects your choice of an opening bid.

♠ A K J x
♡ x x
◇ J x x
♣ K 10 x x

You would open this hand *1 ♣* in first or second seat, keeping the spades in reserve. But in third seat, you don't need to prepare a rebid. Take advantage of the preemptive and lead-directing features of a *1 ♠* opening.

Weak two-bids can solve some of your problems in third seat.

♠ x
♡ K Q J 10 x
◇ J x x
♣ K x x x

You can't open this hand 1 ♡ after two passes — no spade tolerance. You could, however, open *2 ♡* (weak). Your partner will be slightly misled about your heart length, but since he is a passed hand, it isn't likely to matter.

Actually, you would *pass* this hand if you knew that your left-hand opponent would also pass and the hand would be thrown in. Your shortness in spades, the *ranking suit,* is a bad sign.

♠ x
♡ A 10 x x x
◇ K Q x
♣ Q x x x

We suggested a third-seat *pass* on this hand, with no tolerance for the suit in which partner would probably respond. The fact that the suit is spades affords a second argument for passing. With no length in the ranking suit, you prefer that the auction not start at all. If the *opponents* have a fine spade fit, they will outbid you.

Your holding in the ranking suits is the most important consideration in opening borderline hands in *fourth* seat.

♠ x
♡ A J x x
◇ K Q x
♣ Q x x x x

You might open this hand in *first* seat, but you should pass in *fourth* position. There is a clear danger that the opponents have a spade fit and will buy the contract in a competitive auction. You would open with:

♠ A J x x x
♡ Q x x x
◇ K Q x
♣ x

II. PASSED-HAND RESPONSES

There is a special consideration here. Partner is *no longer forced to rebid* if you respond in a new suit. *You may be dropped* in your response if partner has opened a minimum or sub-minimum hand.

In each example partner opened 1 ♡ after two passes.

1. ♠ J x x x   Respond *1 NT*, suggesting a playable con-
    ♡ x x   tract if partner is going to pass. You prefer
    ◇ K 10 x x   a better suit to respond 1 ♠ *as a passed*
    ♣ A J x   hand.

2. ♠ K Q x x   You can safely respond 2 ♣, planning to
    ♡ K x   bid 2 ♠ next. It is true that you will have
    ◇ x x   reversed, but since you are a passed hand,
    ♣ K 10 x x x   partner will not be misled as to your
                  strength.

3. ♠ K x x   Respond 2 NT, showing a hand just short
    ♡ x x   of a normal 2 NT response.
    ◊ A J x x
    ♣ K 10 x x

4. ♠ x x   Respond 3 ♡, showing a hand just short
    ♡ K x x x   of a normal double raise.
    ◊ A x x x
    ♣ K J x

5. ♠ x x   If you weren't a passed hand, you would
    ♡ A J x   have to temporize with 2 ♣ and raise
    ◊ A x x x   hearts later. A direct 3 ♡ bid is better
    ♣ Q 10 x x   here, since you don't want to risk being
                 left in 2 ♣.

6. ♠ x x   Respond 3 ◊. A *jump shift* by a passed
    ♡ K J x x   hand is forcing, shows a fit for partner's
    ◊ A K x x x   suit, and suggests that the hand is im-
    ♣ x x   proved because of partner's opening bid.

III. "PSYCHIC" BIDDING

Some players, not satisfied to open hands that are merely light, like to bid with little or nothing at all! Weak opponents may be intimidated and fail to bid the value of their cards (missing an easy game or slam), and even experienced players may be confused by a "psych" and miss their best contract.

Psychic bids are bluffs, made with the hope of deceiving the opponents. The problem with psychic bidding is obvious. It may be your partner and not the opponents you fool. If you open 1 ♡ with:

    ♠ x x
    ♡ Q J x x x
    ◊ x x x
    ♣ x x x

the opponents may or may not proceed to bid their laydown game; but if your partner has a good hand, you will be sorry you tried such a tactic.

An additional consideration is that *even if your psychic strategy is successful,* you undermine the confidence that any good partnership *must* have. Your partner will begin to wonder what you might be up to every time you bid.

Another drawback to frequent psychics is that they create an unhealthy climate at the table. If partner has seen you "operate" several times, he will be on the lookout for your psychs. This will give your partnership an unfair *edge* in the bidding. In tournament play, where a strict code of ethics is upheld, good results you achieve because partner miraculously figured out that you were fooling around are disallowed.

Psychic bids may get you a good result once in a while, but they are losing tactics in the long run. They are no way to get a reputation as a fine bridge player. It's better to earn a tag as a steady, dependable player who wins through consistently good technique and a sound knowledge of the game.

*LEARNING HOW TO PLAY CARD COMBINATIONS WILL
PUT YOU ON THE WINNING ROAD.*

TEST YOUR COMPREHENSION OF THE MATERIAL IN THIS CHAPTER:

QUIZ ON CARD COMBINATIONS AS DECLARER:

In each of the following card combinations, what is the best play for the number of tricks indicated? There may be more than one problem to each card combination. Assume that the bidding and play have given no useful information. Entries are plentiful.

1. A K 10 x x   FIVE tricks

    J x x

2. A x x x   THREE tricks

    Q J x x

3. A J x x   THREE tricks,
                         TWO tricks
    10 x x x

4. A K 10   THREE tricks

    x x x

5. K 10 9 8   TWO tricks

    x x x x

6. Q 10 x   ONE trick

    x x x

7. A J x x   FOUR tricks,
                         THREE tricks
    K 9 x x

8. A Q 9   THREE tricks

    J x x

9.   ♠ x x x
     ♡ x x x
     ◇ x x x
     ♣ A J x x

     ♠ A K x
     ♡ A K x
     ◇ A x x
     ♣ K 9 x x

10.   ♠ A J x x
      ♡ x
      ◇ K x x
      ♣ Q x x x x

      ♠ x
      ♡ K J 10 x x x x x
      ◇ A x
      ♣ x x

You are declarer with these cards. The opening lead is the ♠Q. How do you play if the contract is:

(a) 2 NT?
(b) 3 NT?

You opened 4♡ as dealer and all passed. The opening lead is the ♠10 and you win dummy's ace. How do you play the trumps?

SOLUTIONS:

1. Play the ace and king.
2. Play the ace and lead low toward the queen-jack.
3. THREE tricks — lead low to the jack. If it loses, play the ace next.
   TWO tricks — play the ace and lead toward the ten.
4. Lead low to the ten, hoping the queen and jack are both onside.
5. Lead low to the eight. If that loses to the queen or jack, lead low to the nine next.
6. Lead to the ten. If the ace or king wins on your right, lead to the queen next.
7. FOUR tricks — lead low to the jack.
   THREE tricks — lead the ace and low toward your hand, planning to play the nine if right-hand opponent follows low on the second round. If left-hand opponent can win this trick, the suit has split evenly. If right-hand opponent has a singleton, win the king on the second lead and lead back toward the jack. This safety play guards against Q-10-x-x with either opponent.
8. Lead the jack; if it is covered, finesse the nine.
9. (a) Take the *safety play* for *three* club tricks. Lead to the ace and back to the nine.
   (b) Lead a club to the jack, hoping for *four* club tricks.

10. Lead a heart to your *king*. This is a guess in principle, but you will gain by playing the king if left-hand opponent has the singleton queen. If left-hand opponent has the singleton ace, you will always lose two tricks.

QUIZ ON "LOOSE ENDS" IN THE BIDDING:

I. You are in third position after two passes. What action do you take with these hands?

1.   ♠ x x
     ♡ Q J x x x
     ◇ A J x
     ♣ Q J x

2.   ♠ x
     ♡ Q 10 x x x
     ◇ K Q x
     ♣ A x x x

3.   ♠ x x
     ♡ A x x
     ◇ A Q x
     ♣ J x x x x

4.   ♠ A Q 10 x x
     ♡ J x x
     ◇ A x x
     ♣ x x

5.   ♠ Q x x
     ♡ A K J x x
     ◇ J x x
     ♣ x x

6.   ♠ J x x
     ♡ J x x
     ◇ K Q 10 x x
     ♣ A x

7.   ♠ A K J x
     ♡ x x
     ◇ Q x x
     ♣ Q 10 x x

8.   ♠ K Q J 10 x
     ♡ x
     ◇ K x x
     ♣ J x x x

9.   ♠ x
     ♡ Q x x
     ◇ A x x x
     ♣ A x x x x

10. ♠ K Q J x x x
     ♡ x x
     ◇ A J x
     ♣ J x

178

II. Partner has opened 1♡ after two passes. Your right-hand opponent passes, and you must respond *as a passed hand*. What action do you take with these hands?

1. ♠ J x x x
   ♡ x x
   ◇ A J x x
   ♣ Q J x

2. ♠ A Q x x
   ♡ Q x
   ◇ x x
   ♣ K x x x x

3. ♠ A Q x
   ♡ x x
   ◇ K 10 x
   ♣ Q 10 x x x

4. ♠ x x
   ♡ A J x x
   ◇ A Q x x
   ♣ x x x

5. ♠ x x
   ♡ A Q x
   ◇ J x x x
   ♣ A x x x

6. ♠ x x
   ♡ K x x x
   ◇ A K J x x
   ♣ x x

7. ♠ x x x
   ♡ K x x
   ◇ K x x
   ♣ A x x x

8. ♠ A K x x x
   ♡ x
   ◇ K x x x
   ♣ J x x

9. ♠ J x x
   ♡ A x x
   ◇ Q 10 x x
   ♣ A J x

10. ♠ A x x
    ♡ x x x
    ◇ Q x
    ♣ K Q x x x

179

SOLUTIONS:

I.   1.   Pass.   You lack the defensive values to open.
     2.   Pass.   You cannot pass a 1♠ response comfortably.
     3.   Pass.   You don't want to suggest a club lead.
     4.   1♠
     5.   1♡
     6.   1♢
     7.   1♠,   since you plan to pass any response.
     8.   2♠,   if playing weak two-bids; otherwise, pass.
     9.   Pass.   Perhaps the hand will be passed out.
    10.   2♠,   if playing weak two-bids; otherwise, 1♠.

II.   1.   1 NT.   You prefer a better suit to respond 1♠ *as a passed hand.*
     2.   2♣,   planning to bid 2♠ next.
     3.   2 NT
     4.   3♡
     5.   3♡.   Avoid a *temporizing* response if you are a passed hand.
     6.   3♢.   Partner's opening has improved your hand.
     7.   2♡   is probably your best response.
     8.   1♠
     9.   2 NT
    10.   2♣.   Risk a temporizing response with your bad hearts.

YOU HAVE REACHED THE FINISH LINE!

COMPREHENSIVE GLOSSARY

"ABOVE THE LINE":	Scoring of points won for overtricks, penalties and bonuses.
ACTIVE DEFENSE:	The defenders' approach when they are desperate for tricks because declarer threatens to get discards for his losers.
ASSUMPTION:	Technique by which declarer or defender bases his play on the premise that the contract can be made or set.
ATTITUDE:	Defensive signal that shows like or dislike for a suit.
AVOIDANCE:	Technique in play whereby a dangerous opponent is kept from gaining the lead.
AUCTION:	See BIDDING.
BALANCED HAND:	Hand containing no void suit or singleton, and no more than one doubleton.
BALANCING:	Backing into the auction after the opponents have stopped low, counting on partner to hold some values.

"BELOW THE LINE":	Scoring of points that count toward making a game.
BID:	Call in the auction that promises to take a certain number of tricks in the play and suggests a suit as trumps (or suggests the play be at notrump).
BIDDING:	The first phase of each hand of bridge, when the players on both sides have a chance to bid for the right to name the trump suit and suggest how many tricks they expect their side to win in the play.
BLACKWOOD:	A conventional bid of 4 NT that asks partner to reveal, through an artificial response, the number of aces he holds.
BOOK:	(1) The first six tricks won by declarer's side; (2) the number of tricks the defenders must win before they begin to score undertricks.
BROKEN SEQUENCE:	Sequence such as QJ9, which contains a gap between the middle and lowest of the three cards.
BROKEN SUIT:	Suit which contains no cards adjacent in rank.
BUSINESS DOUBLE:	Penalty double.
CALL:	Any action, including a pass, taken in the bidding.
CAPTAINCY:	The bidding principle whereby one partner is obliged to take responsibility for placing the contract once his partner's hand is limited in strength.
CARD SENSE:	An intangible quality that those skilled in card play seem to possess.
CHICAGO SCORING:	A type of scoring in which every deal is taken as a separate entity. There are no rubbers or partscores carried over the next deal.
COME-ON:	An encouraging attitude signal.
COMPETITIVE BIDDING:	Auctions in which both sides bid.
CONSTRUCTIVE BIDDING:	Auctions in which one side tries to reach its best contract without interference.
CONTRACT:	The number of tricks that the side that wins the auction undertakes to make.
CONTROL:	Holding that prevents the opponents from taking two fast tricks in that suit. An ace; king; or singleton or void, if some other suit is trumps.
CONVENTION:	A bid to which an artificial meaning has been assigned.
CROSS-RUFF:	A play technique in which cards are trumped in both partnership hands alternately, on several successive tricks.

CUEBID:	(1) A bid of an opponent's suit, intended to show great strength. (2) A bid of a suit in which a control is held, intended to facilitate slam investigation. (3) Any of several conventional cuebids, such as Michaels.
CUT:	The division of the pack into rough halves prior to the deal.
DEAL:	The distribution of the 52 cards, 13 to each player face down, that begins each hand of bridge.
DECLARER:	The player who tries to make the contract by using both his own and dummy's cards.
DEFENDERS:	The partnership that opposes declarer and tries to defeat the contract.
DISCARD:	A played card which is not of the suit led nor of the trump suit.
DOUBLE:	A call generally intended to increase the penalty suffered by the opponents if their last bid becomes an unsuccessful çontract.
DOUBLE FINESSE:	A combination of plays in which declarer finesses against two missing honors.
DOUBLE SQUEEZE:	An advanced type of squeeze in which each defender is squeezed in turn.
DOUBLETON:	A holding of two cards in a suit.
DRAW TRUMPS:	Technique in which declarer leads trumps, forcing the opponents to follow suit, until their trumps are exhausted.
DROP:	Cause a missing high card to fall by playing a still higher card or cards.
DUMMY:	Declarer's partner. The term is also applied to the dummy's cards, placed face up on the table.
DUMMY REVERSAL:	Technique by which declarer makes extra tricks by ruffing several times in his own hand and ultimately drawing trumps with dummy's trump holding.
DUPLICATE BRIDGE:	A contest in which the same hands are played several times by different players, allowing for a comparison of results.
DUPLICATION OF VALUES:	The condition in which the high cards and distribution of the partnership hands are ill-suited to each other.
ECHO:	A high-low sequence of play used to signal attitude or count.
ENDPLAY:	Technique by which a trick is gained through deliberately giving an opponent the lead in a position where he has no safe exit.
ENTRY:	A card used as a means of gaining the lead.
EQUALS:	Cards that are adjacent in rank, or that become adjacent when the cards that separate them are played.

FALSE CARD:	A card played with intent to deceive.
FALSE PREFERENCE:	A preference offered without true support, typically with two cards.
FINESSE:	Maneuver by which it is hoped to win a trick with an intermediate card, by playing that card after one opponent has already played.
FIT:	A holding which suggests that suit will adequately serve as trumps.
FIVE-CARD MAJORS:	A bidding style in which an opening bid of 1 ♠ or 1 ♡ promises five or more cards.
FOLLOWING SUIT:	Each player's first obligation in the play, to play a card of the same suit that was led to the trick if possible.
FORCING BID:	A bid that compels partner to take further action.
FORCING DEFENSE:	The defenders' approach when they try to exhaust declarer of trumps by repeatedly forcing him to ruff.
FORCING PASS:	Pass made over an opponent's bid, which compels partner to double the opponents or bid further.
FREE BID:	Bid made when the alternative would be to pass and allow partner the next opportunity to act. Typically based on sound values.
FREE RAISE:	Raise of partner's suit in competition. Not a significant term, since such a raise does *not* imply extra strength.
GAME:	(1) A unit of scoring, two of which comprise a rubber; a game is won by the first partnership to score 100 or more points below the line. (2) Any contract which will allow the partnership to score game if fulfilled.
GAME TRY:	A bid that suggests interest in game and asks partner to assess his values and make the final decision.
GERBER:	A conventional bid of 4 ♣ that asks partner to reveal, through an artificial response, the number of aces he holds.
GRAND SLAM FORCE:	A bid of 5 NT, when used to show interest in bidding a grand slam in the agreed trump suit provided partner holds certain honors in trumps.
HIGH-CARD POINT COUNT:	Method of hand evaluation in which a numerical value is assigned to each high honor.
HONOR:	Ace, king, queen, jack or ten.
HONORS:	Bonus available in the scoring for a holding of four or all five honors in the trump suit in the same hand; or, at notrump, all four aces in the same hand.
HOLD-UP:	Refusal to take a winner, often for purposes of disrupting the opponents' communication.
INFERENCE:	A conclusion logically deduced from evidence.

INFERENTIAL COUNT:	An assessment of the entire distribution of the concealed hands, based on evidence from the bidding and the early play.
INTERIOR SEQUENCE:	Holding such as KJ109x, in which the equals are accompanied by some higher card.
INTERMEDIATES:	Cards which may become winners as the cards that outrank them are played.
INVITATIONAL BID:	Bid that asks partner to continue to game or slam with maximum values.
JORDAN:	The conventional understanding in which a jump to 2 NT by responder, after the opener's bid is doubled for takeout, shows a limit raise in opener's suit.
JUMP OVERCALL:	A suit bid made usually (as the next bid) after an opponent has opened the bidding, but at a higher level than necessary.
JUMP SHIFT:	(1) A jump of one level in a new suit by opening bidder. (2) A jump of one level in a new suit by responder. Either action implies great strength.
LEG:	A fulfilled partscore, a step toward game.
LEAD:	The first card played to a trick.
LIMIT BID:	Bid that promises no more than a pre-agreed amount of high-card strength.
LIMIT RAISE:	Direct double raise of partner's opening one-bid that promises invitational values only.
LONG CARDS:	Low cards that become winners because they are the only cards of their suit which remain in play.
MAJOR SUITS:	Spades and hearts.
MATCHPOINT SCORING:	Type of scoring used in duplicate (tournament) bridge, in which several different results from an identical deal are compared.
MAXIMUM:	Holding the greatest possible values for one's previous bidding.
MINIMUM:	Holding the fewest possible values for one's previous bidding.
NEGATIVE RESPONSE:	Bid, often artificial, that denies good values; made in response to partner's forcing action.
NOTRUMP:	Strain in which the play is conducted with no trump suit. The highest card played of the suit that is led to a trick wins that trick.
OBLIGATORY FALSECARD:	Falsecard that will lead to a certain loss if not played.
OBLIGATORY FINESSE:	The handling of certain suit combinations in which declarer plays a low card from both hands, hoping his opponent will be forced to follow suit with a high honor.
OFFSIDE:	Unfavorably placed for a finesse to work.

ONSIDE:	Favorably placed for a finesse to work.
OPEN THE BIDDING:	To make the first bid in the auction.
OPENING LEAD:	The lead to the first trick, made by the defender to declarer's left.
OVERCALL:	Bid in a suit after the opponents have opened the bidding (but before partner has taken any action).
OVERTRICKS:	Tricks taken in excess of those bid.
PARTIAL:	A partscore.
PARTNERSHIP:	Two players working as a unit. Bridge is played by two competing partnerships. Partners sit opposite each other. Trust and cooperation between partners are important features of the game.
PARTSCORE:	A contract below the level of game. Successful partscores can accumulate toward scoring game.
PASS:	Call in the auction when the player does not wish to bid, double or redouble.
PASSED OUT:	Deal on which none of the four players bid. Calls for another deal.
PASSIVE DEFENSE:	Defenders' approach when dummy is short of winners and the defense can wait on its tricks.
PENALTY DOUBLE:	Double made for a larger penalty, in the expectation that the contract will fail.
PERCENTAGE PLAY:	Line of play which will succeed most often, determined on only a mathematical basis.
PLAIN SUIT:	Any suit other than trumps.
POINT COUNT:	The method of hand evaluation whereby a numerical value is assigned to the possible trick-taking features of a hand.
POSITIVE RESPONSE:	Response to partner's forcing opening that promises certain good values.
PREEMPTIVE BID:	Bid made not for constructive purposes but merely to crowd the opponents and make it hard for them to bid accurately.
PREFERENCE:	A bid which chooses between two possible strains partner has offered.
PREPARED BID:	An opening bid in a low-ranking suit (often, a suit of only three cards), made so that a higher-ranking suit will provide an easy, space-saving rebid.
PRIMARY VALUES:	Aces and kings.
PROPRIETIES:	That section of the Laws of Contract Bridge that deals with ethics and etiquette.

PSYCHIC BID:	A bluff bid, made on a non-existent suit or without values, intended to intimidate the opposition.
QUANTITATIVE SLAM (GAME) TRY:	Bid that asks partner to pass or bid on, based strictly on the number of high-card values he holds.
RAISE:	A bid in the same suit (or notrump) that partner has just bid, often confirming that suit as trumps.
REBID:	(1) Bid the same suit a second time. (2) Any bid chosen at one's second turn.
REDOUBLE:	Call available in the auction which doubles, in turn, points scored if the contract is played doubled.
RESPONDER:	Opening bidder's partner.
RESTRICTED CHOICE:	A mathematical concept, based on the opponents' possible play from a holding of several equal cards, that may be helpful in determining the play of certain suit combinations.
REVERSE:	(1) A rebid in a new suit, such that the level of the contract will be increased if partner shows a preference for the first suit. (2) To bid in such a way, thereby showing a strong hand.
REVOKE:	Failure to follow suit when holding a card of the suit led.
RUBBER:	Unit of scoring in bridge, won by the side to first make two games, and carrying a large bonus.
RUFF:	To trump.
RUFF-AND-DISCARD (RUFF-SLUFF):	The lead of a suit in which both declarer and dummy are void, allowing declarer to discard a loser from the hand of his choice while he ruffs in the other.
RULE OF 11:	Device, applicable if the lead is known to be fourth-highest, that may be used to make judgments in the play. Subtract the rank of the spot led from 11. The remainder shows the number of higher cards held by the hands, other than leader's.
SACRIFICE:	A deliberate overbid, but one in which declarer expects to be penalized fewer points than the opponents would score if allowed to play their own contract.
SAFETY PLAY:	The handling of a combination of cards so as to insure against a devastating loss of tricks.
SECOND-HAND:	(1) The next player to have a chance to bid after the dealer. (2) The player who plays immediately after a trick is led to.
SECONDARY VALUES:	Queens and jacks.
SEMI-BALANCED HAND:	Hand which is neither balanced nor unbalanced by definition, 2-2-4-5 or 2-2-3-6 pattern.
SEQUENCE:	Three or more cards adjacent in rank, the highest one of which is an honor.

187

SET:	To defeat the contract.
SHORT CLUB:	See PREPARED BID.
SHUT-OUT BID:	A preemptive bid.
SIGNAL:	Any of several conventional understandings through which the defenders can give each other information by means of the card they play.
SIGNOFF:	Bid that suggests that partner pass.
SIMPLE SQUEEZE:	Type of squeeze in which a single opponent is squeezed.
SINGLETON:	A holding of only one card in a suit.
SLAM:	A contract for 12 or 13 tricks, carrying a bonus in the scoring.
SPOT CARD:	Card below the rank of an honor.
SQUEEZE:	Technique, most often used by declarer, in which a defender is forced to relinquish a winner no matter what card he chooses.
STANDARD AMERICAN:	The bidding system most commonly used in America; essentially, the Goren style, with gadgets and refinements added.
STOPPER:	A card or combination of cards certain to produce a trick in a suit.
STRIP:	Play a suit or suits so as to make it impossible for an opponent to lead that suit or lead it safely.
SUIT-PREFERENCE SIGNAL:	Defensive signal which bears no relation to its own suit but shows interest in another, specific suit.
SURROUNDING PLAY:	Maneuver in which a defender breaks a suit by leading a high card that is part of a near-sequential holding.
SYSTEM:	The total framework in which the partnership assigns well-defined meanings to its bids and bidding sequences.
TABLE PRESENCE:	The ability to draw inferences from the extraneous things that happen at the table.
TAKEOUT DOUBLE:	Double that requests partner not to pass but to choose a suit (or notrump) to play in.
TEMPORIZE:	Bid a suit (often, an unplayable suit), in the expectation of supporting partner's suit later. May be required if no immediate raise is appropriate.
TENACE:	An honor or combination of honors which will be most valuable if the holder is fourth-hand to play; e.g., AQ, KJ.
THIRD HAND:	In the auction, dealer's partner. In the play, leader's partner.
THIRD-SEAT OPENING:	An opening bid after two passes that may be based on sub-minimum values. Often it is intended as mainly lead-directing and mildly preemptive.

THROW-IN:	See ENDPLAY.
TRAP PASS:	Pass made with substantial values, including strength in the opponent's suit, in the hope of making a successful penalty double later.
TREATMENT:	A particular way of assigning a natural meaning to a bid or sequence of bids.
TRICK:	Four cards played in sequence, one by each player at the table, going clockwise.
TRUMPS:	The suit determined in the bidding to be that of the contract.
TRUMP CONTROL:	Technique by which declarer makes possession of the trump suit work to his advantage, exhausting the opponents of their trumps so he can safely establish and cash other winners.
TRUMP COUP:	The advanced play by which declarer can avoid losing a trick to an outstanding trump honor by forcing the defender to ruff and be overruffed.
TRUMP ECHO:	The high-low sequence of play in the trump suit, used in defense to show an odd number of trumps.
TRUMP PROMOTION:	Defensive technique in which declarer is forced to either ruff low and be overruffed or ruff high at the later cost of a trick.
TRUMP SUPPORT:	Usually four or more cards in partner's suit. Under some circumstances, three or fewer cards.
UNBALANCED HAND:	Hand containing a void suit or singleton.
UNBLOCK:	Play by declarer or defenders so as to allow the uninterrupted run of a long suit by proper management of the smaller cards.
UNDERTRICKS:	Tricks which declarer has bid but fails to take.
UPPERCUT:	Defensive technique in which a defender ruffs in with a trump intermediate and declarer is obliged to weaken his trump holding by overruffing.
VOID:	A suit in which no cards are held.
VULNERABILITY:	Condition in the scoring, achieved when one game has been won toward completion of the rubber.
WEAK TWO-BID:	Modern treatment in which an opening bid of 2 ♠, 2 ♡ or 2 ◊ shows a good six-card suit and about an average hand in high cards.

— NOTES —

— NOTES —

DEVYN PRESS PUBLICATIONS
BRIDGE BOOKS